ABOUT LOVE

The End of Time

Fortitude and Temperance

Happiness and Contemplation

Leisure the Basis of Culture

Scholasticism

The Silence of St. Thomas

Guide to Thomas Aquinas

Belief and Faith

Enthusiasm and Divine Madness

The Four Cardinal Virtues

In Tune With the World
A Theory of Festivity

ABOUT LOVE

by Josef Pieper

Translated by Richard and Clara Winston

FRANCISCAN HERALD PRESS

1434 WEST 51st STREET   CHICAGO, 60609

Made in the United States of America

Library of Congress Cataloging in Publication Data

Pieper, Josef, 1904-
  About love.

  Translation of Uber die Liebe.
  Includes bibliographical references.
  1. Love.   I. Title.
  BD436.P513   177'.7   74-10905
  ISBN 0-8199-0536-4

For
Michael and Barbara
Pieper

CONTENTS

V

VI

VII

VIII

IX

of enjoyment, not personal union — "The fig leaf moved up in front of the face" — The deceptive character of mere sexuality. Trivialization by making light of; sex without pleasure — Compulsive nature of sex consumption; "totalitarian coldness" — Diabolism and "exorcism." The role of sophistry.

X

Some thoughts on friendship, maternal and paternal love — Reenactment of the Creator's primal affirmation: the basis for an understanding of caritas — Mother Teresa in Calcutta and her "hospital of the dying" — The novelty in this love. What is meant by "for Christ's sake"? — Loving one's fellow men as "companions in future bliss." The common element in caritas and erotic love. — What is natural to love and natural in love is presupposed, but also perfected. Perfection always means transformation as well. Fire as the symbol of love.

Love is the prime gift.
Whatever else is freely
given to us becomes a
gift only through love.

ABOUT LOVE

I

THERE ARE MORE than enough considerations that might keep us from committing ourselves to the subject of love. After all, we need only leaf through a few magazines at the barber's to want not to let the word "love" cross our lips for a good long time. But there is an equal danger lurking in an entirely different quarter, the "triumphal misunderstanding"[1] which unrealistically and exaggeratedly portrays love as pure "unselfishness," and in so doing makes the reality of love evaporate. Still and all, such scruples are primarily a matter of taste and impression. Only after we have overcome them do we find ourselves confronting the true difficulty: the sheer overwhelming vastness of the subject. Are we, in fact, dealing with only one subject? Does the noun "love" cover a single, or approximately single area of meaning — or is it not rather something like an archipelago of extremely varied meanings with no discernible connection among them? Is there anything in common among what the entertainment industry calls "love," and what is called *amour physique* in Stendhal's famous essay, and that "theological virtue" which is usually named together with faith and hope? Again, is not the kind of "love" mentioned in Plato's

Symposium something entirely different? Moreover, no one questions our right to speak of "loving" wine, nature, singing. And is there not an absolute abyss between all that and the Bible's statement that God is love?

If we consider the extensive vocabulary of other languages for this area, we may well ask ourselves whether this difficulty exists primarily for German, which is obliged to include widely different concepts within the single word *Liebe*. A famous German classical scholar[2] has actually called his own language "poor" because it has only a single noun for things that "have nothing to do with each other," whereas the Greeks, the Romans, and the speakers of the Romance languages have a good half a dozen different words at their disposal for "love." One professor of philosophy has attempted to rectify the situation by proposing and even carrying out the absurd suggestion that we at least distinguish between *love¹* and *love²* (to be pronounced "love superscript one" and "love superscript two") but with the proviso that these are not to be understood as "different aspects" of one and the same general 'love.' "[3]

In reality the matter is far less simplistic than it may appear at first glance. First of all, the German language, as soon as we go beyond the confines of nouns and enter the realm of verbs, proves to be not all that poor in vocabulary. Some of the words, in fact, suggest a depth of meaning that is not easily plumbed. What, for example, is the inner significance of *einander leiden mögen?* — which means 'to like," although the literal sense is "to be able or willing to suffer someone." (A somewhat similar meaning is found negatively in the English phrase: "He does not suffer fools gladly.")

Furthermore, in other languages also a single fundamental word apparently underlies all the variety in vocabulary and binds together all special meanings. In Latin, for example, and in the modern languages descended from it, this fundamental word is *amor. Omnis dilectio vel caritas est amor, sed non e converso;*[4] this sentence simply confirms existing usage: that all *dilectio* (*dilection*; the word is now obsolete in English, although *predilection* survives) and all *caritas* (*charité,* charity) is fundamentally *amor* (amour, amore, amor). Thus we must once again wonder whether those seemingly disparate things referred to by the German word *Liebe* and the English word "love" really "have nothing to do with one another." Sigmund Freud on the one hand also speaks of the "carelessness" of language in applying the word *Liebe.*[5] But on the other hand he points out, "In all its whims linguistic usage remains faithful to some kind of reality."[6] Presumably, then, there may be a message hidden within the apparent or alleged "poverty" of the German vocabulary of love. It may be that the language itself is telling us not to overlook the underlying unity in all the forms of love, and to keep this broad common element in mind in the face of all the misuses that result from narrowing down the concept.

Such misuses certainly occur in plenty. Apparently the basic words of any language, words that concern the central issues of existence, are particularly subject to perversion. André Gide at eighty, already too weary to continue his journals, wrote in one of his last notations a few weeks before his death, "Distinction, dignity, greatness — I am afraid and almost embarrassed to employ these words, so shamelessly have they been misused. . . . They might be called obscene words like, moreover, all noble words, starting with the word 'virtue.' "[7] C. S. Lewis has actually called this tendency to invert the meanings of words of ethical praise into their opposite a law: "Give a good quality a name and that name will soon be the name of a defect."[8]

This partly accounts for the shyness that appears to inhibit many persons from pronouncing the shamefully abused word "love." Instead, people prefer to speak of

5

"humanitarianism" or "solidarity." But do not such terms mean something different from "love"? If it is possible to exchange or find substitutes for fundamental words, that is certainly not something that can be done arbitrarily; the process is not susceptible to an act of will, no matter how well founded. On the other hand, it seems perfectly possible to carry the misuse of such a word so far that it will be completely ruined and will simply disappear from usage. The semantic history of the German "love" vocabulary, by the way, offers two striking examples of such occurences. These examples should provoke a good deal more thought than has hitherto been given to them.

Minne, for instance, is a word that was totally eliminated from living German speech because it had been so misused. In the works of medieval poets like Wolfram von Eschenbach and Walther von der Vogelweide, but also in general, nonpoetic usage, *Minne* was "the usual word for love."[9] Thus the German language originally had more than one noun at its disposal. In fact, *Minne* seems to have been the more exacting term, compared to *Liebe*.[10] It signified, according to the Grimm *Deutsches Wörterbuch*,[11] not only man's devoted love for God (*Gottesminne*), but the solicitude accorded those in need of help, and the love between man and woman. But by the year 1200 Walther von der Vogelweide was already complaining that "many a false coin is struck"[12] with the image of *Minne*. The word remained in use for quite a while; but the progressive vulgarization of its meaning eventually had the consequence that employing it "became impossible."[13] Then it was extinguished with a kind of fierceness; it was even replaced in already printed books by pasting the word *Liebe* over it.[14]

In Notker's German psalter written around the year 1000, *Minne* held sway unassailed; for Luther, five hundred years later, the word no longer existed.[15] As the Grimm dictionary laconically observes, it has "been avoided since the sixteenth century and is now obsolete."[16] And so it has remained to the present day. None of the efforts of the romantics and none of the Wagner operas has succeeded in bringing the word back to living speech. Although a new German translation of Kierkegaard by Emmanuel Hirsch[17] attempted to render one of the two Danish expressions for love by *Minne*, that effort has remained an isolated bit of archaizing without any significance for actual contemporary German speech.

The second linguistic episode on which we would briefly report here is the attempt to introduce the word *caritas* into German usage — or, rather, the failure of this attempt. The episode shows how fruitless it is to try to control a living language and to overcome its supposed "poverty" by deliberate correction. In this case the intention was to set off the special aspect of love as a theological virtue in contrast to whatever else language calls by the name of "love." Granted, at this point another and even more far-reaching problem enters in, that of "language and terminology" — the historically evolved word as distinct from the artificial technical term. Of course there can be no objection to using more or less artificial terminology in technical discussions, in the interest of greater accuracy. Thus, for example, there is nothing wrong with the theologian's using the term *caritas* in order to define more precisely the supernatural love of God and neighbor. And as long as this technical expression is distinguished from ordinary speech, and is kept apart from it, everything is "quite all right." But if it is introduced into general usage, or adapted, it is flung into the dynamic processes of living language and inevitably runs the risk of semantic change, of narrowing of meaning, and of becoming worn out. What is more, the danger to such technical terms seems greater than to words that have evolved naturally or have been created by poets in the spirit of the language.

Precisely this is what happened when the word *caritas* moved from a technical expression in theological discourse to a quasi-German loan-word, *Karitas*.[18] The meaning of these two words has ceased to be identical. *Karitas* (much like "charity" in English) now means, principally if not exclusively, organized care for those in need, together with the necessary apparatus (associations, offices, directors, etc.). Again we must say that of course there can be no objection to this; on the contrary, the shift in meaning in one sense expresses a fine and praiseworthy thing. What is more, who would venture to deny that in most cases the love of God and love of neighbor is at work, more or less hidden, in the administration of charity. Still, what theological precept has always meant by *caritas* is something quite different and far more. When we give thought to this, it is no longer hard to see that Karl Jaspers should place "charity" and "love" in opposition and can speak of the possibility of "charity without love."[19] In the thirties there were efforts — probably under the influence of Anders Nygren's book *Eros und Agape* — to introduce the Biblical Greek term *agape* into general usage in German. Had this been more successful, the word would sooner or later have probably suffered a similar fate.

But whether or not the immediately available stock of words is "poor" or "rich" — what is far more crucial is for us to grasp as much as we can of the multiplicity of the phenomenon we call "love." This can be done only by an interpretation of both our own language and of foreign languages, to the extent that they are accessible to us — which they may or may not be even when we "know" them. The fragmentary and haphazard nature of such attempts at interpretation is as self-evident as it is unavoidable. I am convinced that not even the matter that everybody means and "knows" in our own daily speech can be translated into exact, carefully considered phraseology without something's being omitted. In addition, we can scarcely count on perceiving the overtones and reverberations of living usage in other languages, not to mention "dead" ones. And of course we realize that no one ever obtains a working knowledge of more than a tiny fraction of the languages that have actually been spoken on our planet, including present-day living languages. Nevertheless, keeping in mind the incompleteness and the accidental character of our information, we may still say that we learn quite a good deal about the phenomenon of "love" by carefully considering the vocabulary associated with it.

Latin, the "ancient" language that up to the present day has made the most vital contributions to the vocabulary of the nations of Europe, had at least half a dozen words to signify love. *Amor* and *caritas* are generally known. But the Christian acts of love which nowadays are lumped under the heading of *caritas* ("charity"), were called by the contemporaries of St. Augustine acts of *pietas*, as he himself relates.[20] *Dilectio*, a fourth word, has already been mentioned in passing. But we must include in this same category not only *affectio*, but also and rather unexpectedly *studium*. It has even been said[21] that this very word expresses an aspect of loving concern that was particularly characteristic of the Romans, namely the desire to serve and to be "at the service of." This does indeed point out something seldom specified as part of love, but that everyone agrees belongs to the full realization of love.

Pietas, too, it appears, points to an element in the whole picture of love which is not immediately apparent. Granted, it can scarcely be said that an essential (and therefore permanent) element of love is something like pity (from *pietas*!), although Arthur Schopenhauer so argued with a radicality that plainly distorted the actuality, "All true and pure love is pity."[22] But the Latin word does rightly suggest that real love "cannot be without mercifulness."[23]

The term *affection* introduces still another of the semantic elements in "love"; the word has passed into French and English virtually unchanged in appearance and meaning. The element is that of *passio*, which here means neither passion nor suffering but the passive nature of love. For despite the active grammatical form, everyone knows that loving is not exclusively, and perhaps not even primarily, something that we ourselves actively do. It is additionally and perhaps much more deeply something that happens to us. Goethe at sixty remarked in conversation, "Love is suffering . . . You have to put up with it; you don't seek it."[24] Although he could claim a certain competence on the subject of love, this was probably something of an exaggeration. Yet the question remains: Who, strictly speaking, is the active subject when someone "pleases" us or when we find someone "enchanting." Ordinary usage, at any rate, would scarcely term it truly human love if the "lover" displayed, no matter how heroically unselfish he might be, nothing but consciously directed (inner or outer) activity, but not a grain of passivity, no sign of having been *affected*.

On the other hand, of course, no one fails to recognize that the passively blind process of spontaneously "being pleased" cannot be everything, that an element of probing judgment and selective preference enters in. Love that comes from the center of existence, engaging the whole human being, essentially implies *diligere* also. The word means electing and selecting. In Latin and the languages derived from it *dilectio* (*dilection*) seems to be an indispensable word in the vocabulary of love — indispensable in defining the personal, mental quality of human love. In the purely sensual realm *dilectio* naturally has no place, whereas the word *amor*, as Thomas[25] says, embraces the sensual and the mental, and even the spiritual and supernatural elements.

The word *caritas*, too, as its basic meaning indicates,

pertains to an act that can be performed only in the mind, namely evaluation.[26] (*Caritas* incidentally is not at all, as might be thought, a distinctively Christian coinage, but also is part of living usage in classical Latin, for example in Cicero.[27]) We use the related adjective *carus* to denote what is "dear" to us, what we are prepared to pay a high price for. This curious ambiguity occurs in many languages (in Latin, German, French and English, for example), identifying what is beloved with what is expensive. What this suggests is worth noting: for it brings up the question of whether union with the — really or only supposedly — beloved means enough to the lover for him to be willing to pay something for it, and if so how much. Here it seems to me, the essence of all true love, and particularly of the love for God (specifically called *caritas*) which so resists our probing, is actually expressed. We sometimes doubt whether we can possibly "love" God, since He is inaccessible to our emotions. But the word itself tells the questioner that *caritas* is not just something sentimental, nor does it primarily refer to a special intensity of feeling. Rather, it suggests the extremely "solid" and sober matter of evaluation and of readiness if need be to pay something for the union with God. This is the metallic core of *caritas*. The extent to which its radiations can reach out to and penetrate the realm of emotion and even of sensuality is frequently manifested, especially in those who have founded their lives upon *caritas* in the contemporary sense of charity. This is the reason, I think, that St. Francis de Sales in the title of his magnificent treatise on divine love speaks neither of *charité* nor *dilection*. Instead he calls it, with an explicit justification,[28] "*Traité de l'amour de Dieu.*" And *amor* (*amour*) is, once again, nothing more nor less than the German word *Liebe* or the English word *love*: the one word which includes all the dimensions. If St. Francis really gives particular emphasis to any single aspect, it is to the aspect of being carried away, of being kindled to an ardor that actually has physical effects.

Like all living languages, of course, Latin tended to blur the neatly defined boundaries between the areas of meaning covered by different nouns. St. Augustine, for example, had a fine sense of linguistic nuances and himself sometimes spelled out the differences (for example between *amor* and *dilectio*[29]). Yet he was inclined to stress the common element underlying all the forms of love. In the Bible too, he remarks,[30] the words *amor, dilectio, caritas* basically mean the same thing. The Vulgate in fact translates the Greek words *agápe* and *agapan* without differentiation, it appears, by *amor, caritas, dilection,* and by *diligere* as well as *amare*.[31]

Eros: this Greek word which has been taken into all European languages is far more ambiguous than it is usually represented. From even a casual reading of the Platonic dialogues we begin to see how wide its range of meaning is. Affection kindled by physical beauty; intoxicated Godsent madness (*theia mania*); the impulse to philosophical contemplation of the world and existence; the exaltation which went with the contemplation of divine beauty — Plato calls all these things "eros." In Sophocles, moreover, the word is used to mean approximately "passionate joy."[32] The fact that this passage introduces into the very meaning of *eros* the essential relationship of love and joy is an achievement that should never be forgotten or lost; we shall have occasion to speak of it again.

Philia, usually too narrowly translated by "friendship," seems like its related verb *philein* to stress chiefly fellow-feeling, the solidarity among human beings, and not only of friends but also of spouses, fellow-countrymen and people in general. "It is my nature to join in love, not hate" — in this famous sentence of Antigone she speaks neither of *eros* nor of *agape*; the word used is *philein*.[33] *Agape* as a substantive first came into common usage in Biblical Greek. Karl Barth conjectures that the New Testament (as was likewise the case, incidentally, with the Septuagint, the pre-Christian Greek translation of the Old Testament) might have taken up this term precisely because (somewhat along the lines of English *to like*) it had been "a relatively colorless word."[34] Richard Reitzenstein, the philogist and historian of religion, says that in classical Greek *agape* was not reckoned "among literary words."[35] *Storgé* for example, was "literary"; it meant principally familiar love; so was *philanthropia*, which meant primarily benevolent kindness but was also used for love between the sexes. We might also mention *philadelphia*, a late word for brotherly love which like *philanthropia* entered the Greek of the New Testament.[36] But these are of no further concern to us. *Eros* and *agape* remain more important, as the words that with presumably mutually exclusive intent rally the sides and determine the character of the philosophical and theological disputation in which we mean to intervene vigorously in the course of the following pages.

But for the moment we must attempt to formulate a question whose answer, it is true, can only become apparent at the conclusion of this book. But the question itself comes to the fore now, arising from a peculiarity in the Biblical use of *agape*. I am referring to what may be called the "absolute" use of this word, for instance in the sentence: "He who fears is not perfected in love" (1 Jn 4:18). In love *with whom*, we are inclined to ask; or should it be: in the love *of whom*? Certainly a subject and also an object of love are intended. But the sentence is framed as if to imply that something like a new personal quality, the trait of "being in love," exists and fundamentally affects man's relationship to the universe. But as we have said, the precise nature of this quality, and whether it may be posited as an actual potentiality of man, can at best be dealt with at the end of our discussion. Perhaps it will turn out that an answer to this question *is* the conclusion of the book.

The reader who pauses at this point and looks back for

a moment will possibly note a curious omission from our rapid inventory: Does *sex* really not have a place in the classical vocabulary of love? That would certainly be a matter for astonishment — all the more so since any "puritanical" taboos would scarcely have prevailed; we need only think of the blunt language of Aristophanes, Plautus, Terence, and so on. What then is the case? I shall limit myself to quoting an American writer, the author of important works of cultural anthropology, "The curious thing to our ears is how rarely the Latins speak of *sexus*. Sex, to them, was no issue; it was *amor* they were concerned about. Similarly, everyone knows the Greek word *eros*, but practically no one has ever heard of their term for 'sex.' It is *phylon* . . . a zoological term."[37] With a glance at our contemporary situation the same writer advances the thesis: "We are in flight from eros — and we use sex as the vehicle for the flight."[38] But here we are already anticipating a subject that in any case must be discussed at length.

Our review of the English and French vocabularies need not be long — all the more so since (of course) the most important words of the Latin language recur in these languages, with slightly altered meanings (*amour, dilection, charité, charity, affection*). Still, we must mention a few points that enrich and complete the concept of "love."

For example, we very quickly encounter the English distinction between "to like" "to love." A schoolboy, C. S. Lewis comments, is chided for saying of strawberries, "I love them."[39] But if he is "passionately fond" of them, usage permits the phrase. And yet it is not, strictly speaking, the intensity of the emotion that makes for the distinction. Rather, entirely different modes of emotion are involved. Moreover, "to like" can also be applied to a person, but "to love" refers to the more committed "real" love that is directed toward the other's self. It is of course perfectly possible to say of someone, "I like him but I do not love him." In the context of our discussion, however, the converse and equally conceivable case is more important: that it is possible to love someone although there are many things about him that one does not "like." Hence the irrelevance of the argument that it is impossible to like everybody, so how can we possibly obey the commandment to love our neighbor. But then what is meant by loving? That is preisely our question.

I have long been fascinated by two other aspects of the English vocabulary of love. One is the identiy of the words "to like" and "likeness." To be sure, etymologists hold that the words are not at all identical, that they come from entirely different roots; and since I was unable to check this assertion, I let the matter rest. But then an excellent dictionary[40] called my attention to the fact that *amor* and *amare* have something to do "with the radical notion of likeness." More specifically, they are related to the Greek *háma* ("at the same time"), the Latin *similis* and English *same*.[41]

Our concern here, as is the case with our whole effort to survey the vocabulary, is not with the etymological oddity. It is rather with what we can learn from these close relationships about the secret link between "love" and "likeness." The relationship is a more or less concealed one, and yet it does not surprise us. On the contrary, it brings to the fore a long suspected and almost consciously known semantic element: that "love" includes and is based upon a pre-existent relation between the lover and the beloved; that, in other words, no one could love anyone or anything were not the world, in a manner hard to put into words, a single reality and one that can be experienced as fundamentally characterized by unity — a world in which all beings at bottom are related to one another and from their very origins exist in a relationship of real correspondence to one another. In short, we are confirmed in our sensing that love not only yields and

15

creates unity, but also that its premise is unity. Paul Tillich has actually included this state of affairs in his defintion of love. Love, he says, is not so much the union of those who are strangers to one another as the *re*union of those who have been alienated from one another. But alienation can exist only on the basis of a pre-existing original oneness.[42]

For a long time the original meaning of the phrase "to be fond of" seemed to me another riddle of English usage. And what was meant by "a fond look"? That, of course, is the naive question of a non-linguist; still, among my English and Amercian friends I have found hardly any who could answer it. It was therefore a surprise to me to learn that in Middle English *fond* was spelled *fonned* and was thus a disguised past participle derived from an obsolete verb that meant something like enchant or bewitch. To be fond of and fondness therefore suggest "a kind of fascination of the mind"[43] — which once again recalls the passive nature of love as something suffered. Once more the question arises: Are we, when we love, not so much active ourselves as stirred, changed, moved by something lovable? Is love primarily (or only immediately, at the first moment) rapture over the beloved, being rapt by the beloved? Etymologically, rapture means carrying someone away, forcibly transporting him out of himself.[44] That is pretty much a circumlocution for the meaning of the Latin noun *affectio*.

In French this word *affection* actually seems to signify the comprehensive category under which all the various forms of love are subsumed. If we look up the word *amour* in a French dictionary we will find love "in general" characterized as an *affection profonde*, whereas erotic love in the narrower sense is defined as a *sentiment d'affection* of one sex for the other.[45]

To conclude this inevitably more or less haphazard inquiry into vocabulary and usage, let me add two remarks about *Russian* (for which I am wholly dependent upon information from others). They concern two remarkable, so it seems to me, peculiarities in the Russian language's vocabulary of love.

First of all, Russian has a word (*lubovatsia*) that seems to mean approximately "to love with the eyes"[46]: a form of loving that becomes a reality through seeing. The perspectives that unexpectedly come to mind seem infinite. Plato and all philosophies derived from him maintain that the quality that makes a thing the object of possible love is *beauty*. "Only the beautiful is loved"; "we cannot help loving what is beautiful" — these are two statements by St. Augustine.[47] If this is true, and if the old definition is also right: *pulchrum est quod visu placet*, to be beautiful means to be "pleasing to sight"[48] — then evidently there can be no true love without approving contemplation, without a looking that as yet is not tinged with the desire to possess. And it is the achievement of the Russian language to bring this aspect of the phenomenon of love to consciousness by having a special term, a word which in itself is lovable, for the concept "to love with the eyes."

The second Russian peculiarity pierces even more deeply into the matter. Usage involves not only what is actually said but also the impossibility of employing a word in certain contexts — linguistic taboos, as it were. In this connection it has been pointed out, on the basis of an analysis of Latin usage, that it evidently never occurred to the Romans that the gods could "love" men.[49] Now, although the dictionaries published within the country after the October Revolution of 1917 repress the fact,[50] the Russian language has a word (*blágost*) for this very concept: the love of God for men! So here is still another semantic element which must be considered by anyone hoping to grasp the concept, and above all the reality of "love," in its full breadth and depth.

II

If according to the many voices of language love is both something that we "practice" and do as conscious actors, and also something that comes over us and happens to us like an enchantment; if on the one hand it is an emotion directed toward possessing and enjoying, and on the other hand a gesture of self-forgetful surrender and giving which precisely "does not seek its own advantage"; if it is a turning toward someone, possibly God, or other human beings (a friend, a sweetheart, a son, an unknown who needs our help), but possibly also toward the manifold good things of life (sports, science, wine, song); if, finally, it is an act that is ascribed to God Himself and even in a certain sense is said to be identical with Him ("God is love") — if all this is so, does it not seem rather improbable that any kind of common element can be assumed to lie behind all these phenomena? In other words, is there any meaning at all to the universal question: What is the "nature" of love? On the other hand, we are inclined to feel from the start that the fact of there being one single word for all this cannot be entirely without some foundation in reality. But if the recurrent identity underlying the countless forms of love does exist, how can it be more exactly described?

My tentative answer to this question runs as follows: In every conceivable case love signifies much the same as approval. This is first of all to be taken in the literal sense of the word's root: loving someone or something means finding him or it *probus*, the Latin word for "good." It is a way of turning to him or it and saying, "It's good that you exist; it's good that you are in this world!"

To avert possible misunderstandings we must elaborate, and almost correct, this definition. I do not mean that the act of love necessarily involves any such bare statement, although that is quite possible. The approval I am speaking of is rather an expression of the *will*. It signifies the opposite of aloof, purely "theoretical" neutrality. It testifies to being in agreement, assenting, consenting, applauding, affirming, praising, glorifying and hailing. Distinct as the difference in intensity is between mere agreement and enthusiastic affirmation, there is one common element in all the members of this series — which, of course, could easily be extended. All the members are without exceptions forms of expression of the will. All of them mean: I want you (or it) to exist! Loving is therefore a mode of willing. If we are somewhat taken aback at this point, to put it mildly, that is due to the narrow conception of willing impressed upon us by certain philosophical and psychological doctrines. We have been taught to restrict the concept of willing to the idea of willing *to do*, in compliance with a much-quoted definition stating that "real willing" means "deciding in favor of actions on the basis of motives."[1] Such activistic restriction has, quite characteristically, also been applied to the concept of knowing — as though knowing consisted solely in the "rational work" of logical thinking and not just as much in the form of "simple intuition" in which we are immediately certain of precisely the fundamental subjects of thinking, such as existence.[2] Thinking is "discursive" — still on the "course" to its own proper result; it is, we might put it, knowledge of what is absent. But what the thinking mind is still seeking the intuiting mind has already found; it is present to it and before its gaze; its eye "rests" upon it. Seeing, intuiting, in contrast to thinking has, it has been said,[3] no "tension towards the future."

Precisely in the same way there is a form of willing which does not aim at doing something still undone, and thus acting in the future to change the present state of affairs. Rather, in addition to willing-to-do there is also a purely affirmative assent to what already is, and this assent is likewise without "future tension"; *le consentement est sans futur.*[4] To confirm and affirm something already accomplished — that is precisely what is meant by "to love." It is true that the will, as Thomas Aquinas once remarks, is usually called a "striving force," *vis appetitiva.* "But the will knows not only the act of striving for what it does not yet have, but also the other act: of loving what it already possesses, and rejoicing in that."[5] A French commentator on Thomas actually distinguishes, in keeping with this pronouncement, between the will as a "force of love" (*puissance d'amour*) and the will as a force for deciding upon choices.[6]

But this equating of willing and loving is not only to be found in the speculations of a more or less specialized literature; it also occurs in ordinary speech. For example, Jerome's Latin Psalter undoubtedly represents occidental linguistic usage just as much as it helped create that usage. Many times[7] Jerome puts it that God "wills" man (Psalm 18:19), "The Lord has brought me forth into a broad place. He delivered me because he willed me." *Quoniam voluit me* — That is quite legitimately rendered in the translation of the Benedictines of Beuron abbey,[8] "Because he loves me." Martin Buber in his translation of the psalms also plays upon the erotic meaning of love, "He has fetched me out into the broad places; he unlaces me, for he has pleasure in me."

But it does not suffice to say that aside from willing-to-do there is "also" love as one among several possible forms of willing, just as alongside of thinking there is "also" seeing as a mode of knowing. Rather, in the great tradition of European thinking about man it has always been held that just as the immediate certainties of seeing are the foundation and prerequisite of all intellectual activity, so also love is the primal act of willing which permeates all willing-to-do from its very source. It is asserted that all volitional decision has its origin in this fundamental act, that loving is the underlying principle of willing and comes first both in temporal succession and order of rank. Not only, it is held, is love by its nature the earliest act of will,[9] and not only is every impulse of the will derived from love,[10] but love also inspires, as the *principium*,[11] that is as the immanent source, all specific decisions, and keeps them in motion.

It is immediately apparent that here we are asserting something that strikes at the root of the whole structure of existence. For if it is true that all beings at the core are nothing but will[12] and if the will, of all the forces of the psyche, is the dominant and most powerful force,[13] then love as the primal act of the will is simultaneously the point of origin and the center of existence as a whole. What kind of person one is will be decided at this point.[14] *Ex amore suo quisque vivit, vel bene vel male* — "Whether for good or evil, each man lives by his love."[15] It is his love and it alone which must be "in order" for the person as a whole to be "right" and good. There is, says Augustine,[16] a very brief definition of virtue (and "virtue" means nothing but "human rightness"): *virtus est ordo amoris.*

Now, however, we are not speaking of virtue and of rightness, but of the fact that love is an act, in fact the primal act, of the will. But what is it that I really "will" by loving? What do I want when I turn to another person and say: It's good that you exist? It is clear, as has already been noted, that this can be said and meant with very different kinds of orchestration. *In concreto* many different degrees of intensity are conceivable. Still, even the weakest degree evidently testifies to approval of the mere existence of the other person; and that certainly is no small thing. We need only try to answer with complete sincerity the test question: Do I really in my heart of hearts have "nothing against" (this being probably the minimal degree of approval) the existence of this particular, unique associate, neighbor, or housemate? And to move from that to: "How wonderful that you exist!" In saying that, what do I really have in mind? What am I really getting at? What precisely is it that I am "willing"?

Such writers as Thomas Aquinas, Ortega y Gasset, Vladimir Soloviev, and Maurice Blondel have replied to this question with astonishing unanimity in basic intent, although the radicality of some of their statements sometimes makes their point too strongly and renders their answers of dubious value if not downright wrong. Thomas Aquinas in his now famous beginner's textbook avers: The first think that a lover "wills" is for the beloved to exist and live.[17] "The 'I' who loves above all wants the existence of the 'You.' "[18] The somewhat forgotten phenomenologist and logician Alexander Pfänder, a magnificient analyst of the mental processes, calls love "an act of partisanship for the existence of the beloved,"[19] and even "a continual affirmative keeping the beloved in existence";[20] the lover "confers upon the beloved the right to exist on his own authority."[21]

It is true that we read these last two sentences with a feeling of uneasiness; something seems to be wrong. Is this not sentimentally overestimating the powers of a loving person? Ortega y Gasset, although basically intending to make the same point, puts it much more precisely and circumspectly: As lovers, he says, we "continually and intentionally give life to something which depends on us."[22] The lover "refuses to accept the possibility of a universe without it.[23] Maurice Blondel boldly asserts: "*L'amour est par excellence ce qui fait être*"[24] — love is above all what "makes be," that is, what makes something or someone exist. But again we can accept this sententious phrase only if we understand it as bespeaking the lover's *intention*.

By far the most extreme formulation of the idea that is struggling to emerge through all these different phrases is to be found in Vladimir Soloviev's essay "On the meaning of Sexual Love,"[25] in which he describes love as a force that excludes death, protests against it, and actually denies it. I confess that I react to such a statement with perplexed astonishment. Perhaps we may say that true love makes us realize, more directly than any theorizing can, that the beloved as a person cannot simply drop out of reality, and even — though this to be sure will be evident only to the believer — the beloved will be physically resurrected and live forever, through death and beyond it. This at any rate, is the way I have always understood Gabriel Marcel's moving words: "To love a person means to say: You will not die."[26] This is certainly "partisanship for the existence of the beloved";[27] a more intense partisanship cannot be conceived. But does it make sense to say of human love, as Vladimir Soloviev does, that is excludes death and that the inevitability of dying is "incompatible with true love"?[28] That, it seems to me, is crossing a boundary that might almost be called the border with madness.

In a trenchant and witty phrase, Nietzsche has said, "There is always some madness in love; but there is also always some sense in madness."[29] Thus, at least a grain of truth may be detected in all these hyperboles, even in

Soloviev's concept. Starting from such different bases, all these attempts to describe phenomenologically what love is really about ascribe to it the power to sustain existence (keeping the beloved in being; conferring the right to exist; giving existence; and even annullment of death and mortality). Certainly the fact that they all agree on this should cause us to reflect. Granted, these statements tend rashly to overlook the limits imposed upon finite man. Nevertheless, they all bring into the range of vision an aspect of reality that is worth considering. More precisely, two aspects are involved.

First, let us remember that "the most marvellous of all things a being can do is to be."[30] Existence itself, *la presence effective dans le monde*,[31] this simple "act" of being in existence — this being which is so completely incomprehensible and subject to no definition whatsoever, is conferred upon us and all other beings by love and by love alone. And precisely this is what we know and corroborate when we ourselves love. For what the lover gazing upon his beloved says and means is *not*: How good that you are *so* (so clever, useful, capable, skillful), but: It's good that you are; how wonderful that you exist!

Second, the other element in these claims which remains true in spite of the seeming frenzy of the statements is this: that in fact the most extreme form of affirmation that can possibly be conceived of is *creatio*, making to be, in the strict sense of the word. "Creation is the comparative of affirmation."[32] And I am convinced that no one more fully appreciates this, no one is more persuaded of it beyond all argumentation and proof, than the true lover. He "knows" that his affirmation directed toward the beloved would be pointless were not some other force akin to creation involved — and, moreover, a force not merely preceding his own love, but one which is still at work and which he himself, the loving person, participates in and helps along by loving. Granted, such intimations would immediately lose all credence if they seriously tried to attribute to any human being, no matter how passionate or heroic a lover he might be, any really creative power in the strict sense. It is God who in the act of creation anticipated all conceivable human love and said: I will you to be; it is good, "very good" (Gn 1:31) that you exist. He has already infused everything that human beings can love and affirm, goodness along with existence, and that means lovability and affirmability.[33] Human love, therefore, is by its nature and must inevitably be always an imitation and a kind of repetition of this perfected and, in the exact sense of the word, *creative* love of God. And perhaps the lover is not unaware of this, before reflecting at all. How otherwise, for example, can we understand what is perhaps too rarely considered: that even the very first stirrings of love contain an element of gratitude? But gratitude is a reply; it is knowing that one has been referred to something prior, in this case to a larger frame of universal reference which supercedes the realm of immediate empirical knowledge.

Now, however, the "but" must follow the "yes." Yes, all humon love is an echo of the divine, creative, prime affirmation by virtue of which everything that is — including therefore what we *in concreto* love — has at once received existence and goodness. *But*: if all goes happily as it should, then in human love something *more* takes place than mere echo, mere repetition and imitation. What takes place is a continuation and in a certain sense even a perfecting of what was begun in the course of creation.

III

But then, if a human being already exists anyhow, could we not say that it does not matter whether a lover finds it wonderful and affirms it? Does it really add or take away anything that someone says, "It's good that you exist?"

It is clear that in asking this question, which sounds so extremely "realistic," we are basically asking what is the "function" of love within the whole of existence; what it is supposed to do and accomplish in the world. It is one and the same question that we have to answer at this point. But in order to answer this it admittedly does not suffice to analyze, no matter how precisely, the lover's intention and what is "really" willed and meant by the one who feels loving concern. We must move across to the other shore, that is, we must examine the matter from the point of view of the person who happens to be loved. What is really taking place on his side? Soberly considered, what does it mean for a person that another turns to him and says (or thinks, or experiences), "It's good that you exist?"

On this matter let me first give the floor to Jean Paul Sartre, a writer from whom we should have expected a radically different answer from the one he actually gives. According to the "theory" he has systematically developed, every human being is in principle alien to every other, who by looking at him threatens to steal the world from him; everyone is a danger to everyone else's existence, a potential executioner. But fortunately, the creative artist in Sartre, or simply the brilliant observer and describer of human reality, repeatedly rises up against merely intellectual theses. And the artist in him, altogether unconcerned about his own "philosophy," will then say things like this: "This is the basis for the joy of love. . . : we feel that our existence is justified."[1] As may be seen, that is not so very far from the above-mentioned notions of "giving existence" and "conferring the right to exist." Here, however, the matter is seen not from the lover's point of view, but from that of the beloved. Obviously, then, it does not suffice us simply to exist; we can do that "anyhow." What matters to us, beyond mere existence, is the explicit confirmation: It is *good* that you exist; how wonderful that you are! In other words, what we need over and above sheer existence is: to be loved by another person. That is an astonishing fact when we consider it closely. Being created by God actually does not suffice, it would seem; the fact of creation needs continuation and perfection by the creative power of human love.

But this seemingly astonishing fact is repeatedly confirmed by the most palpable experience, of the kind that everyone has day after day. We say that a person "blossoms" when undergoing the experience of being loved; that he becomes wholly himself for the first time; that a "new life" is beginning for him — and so forth. For a child, and to all appearances even for the still unborn child, being loved by the mother is literally *the* precondition for its own thriving. This material love need not necessarily be "materialized" in specific acts of beneficence. What is at any rate more decisive is that concern and approval which are given from the very core of existence

— we need not hesitate to say, which come from the heart, — and which are directed toward the core of existence, the heart, of the child. Only such concern and approval do we call real "love." The observations of René Spitz[2] have become fairly well known. He studied children born in prison, and brought up in scarcely comfortable outward conditions by their imprisoned mother. These he compared with other children raised without their mothers, but in well-equipped, hygienically impeccable American infants' and children's homes by excellently trained nurses. The result of the comparison is scarcely surprising: in regard to illness, mortality and susceptibility to neuroses, the children raised in prison were far better off. Not that the nurses had performed their tasks in a merely routine matter and with "cold objectivity." But it is simply not enough to be able to eat to satiation, not to freeze, to have a roof overhead and everything else that is essential to life. The institutionalized children had all such needs satisfied. They received plenty of "milk"; what was lacking was — the "honey." This allusion to the Biblical metaphor of the "land flowing with milk and honey" (Ex 3:8) is to be found in the masterly essay by Erich Fromm, *The Art of Loving*,[3] which has had unusual success as a book. (That success may have had something to do with a misunderstanding assiduously furthered by the publisher's advertising,[4] which almost kept me from reading the excellent *opusculum*.) Milk, Erich Fromm says,[5] is meant as the quintessence of everything a person requires for allaying the mere needs of life; but honey is the symbol for the sweetness of life and the happiness of existing. And this is precisely what comes across when we are told what the children in the institutions apparently never heard: How good that you exist!

Incidentally, Erich Fromm continues,[6] among people as a whole, not just children, we can very well distinguish those who have received only the milk from those who have received both milk and honey.

When we consider this, what has been said about the creativity of human love also suddenly acquires a wholly new-founded meaning. In human love the creative act of the Deity in establishing existence is continued — so that one who is consciously experiencing love can say, "I need you in order to be myself . . . In loving me you give me myself, *you let me be*."[7] Put differently, "What being-loved makes being do is precisely: be."[8] Of course such language can be misunderstood, as we have said, and can be quite wrong if it is taken "absolutely." But what all such phrases quite rightly express is that man succeeds in fully "existing" and feeling at home in the world only when he is "being confirmed"[9] by the love of another. Above all, the ability to love, in which our own existence achieves its highest intensification, presupposes the experience of being loved by someone else.

Incidentally, Erich Fromm's little book also explicitly speaks of the creation of man by God — with that magnificent lack of embarrassment which it would seem a European achieves only under the influence of the intellectual climate of the American continent. According to Genesis, God did not simply make the universe and man exist. He gave man instead a taste of the honey as well as the milk; that is, He specifically confirmed their existence and literally declared it "good, very good."[10] Now it cannot be altogether unimportant to man's being-in-the-world whether or not he is able to experience himself and his existence as something approved in so absolute a manner. To so experience it he must, of course, think of himself and the world as *creatura*. Whether this is an assumption that can be justified only by faith, or whether it can also be supported and explained by rational arguments (which I happen to think it can be), is a question that need not be explored here.

In any case, the conviction that the universe has been created cannot possibly remain confined to any one special "sector" of existence — not if it is to be anything more than an abstract tenet carried around in the head. We can't just file it away in a "philosophical-religious" pigeonhole. Once it has been thought through to the end, consistently and vitally, it inevitably affects our entire sense of being. For it then follows that all of reality (things, man, we ourselves) presents itself to us as something creatively conceived, something designed, hence something that had a distinct purpose from the start (an idea that, as is well known, Jean Paul Sartre passionately repudiated[11]). Above all we have then to view all reality, again including ourselves, as something creatively willed and affirmed, whose existence depends solely on being so affirmed and loved.

Once we perceive this context, we are awakened to the full meaning of a dictum that long ago degenerated into a sterile schoolbook text: the statement of the existential goodness of all things (*omne ens est bonum*). Augustine says in the last chapter of his *Confessions*, "We see things because they exist; but they exist because Thou seest them."[12] There is an analogous principle at work in our context: Because God wills and affirms things, man and the universe as a whole, therefore and solely for this reason they are good, which is to say lovable and affirmable, to us also.

We have, however, drifted once more into somewhat abstract and general realms. But instead of addressing ourselves to the enormous implications of this thought, let us rather consider what the concrete experience of being ourselves approved by the Creator might possibly mean. What really matters here is the living experience. In the example of René Spitz, the mothers' love, no matter how heartfelt, would be no help at all to the small children if they could not be reached in some way, if they did not "know" that they were loved. In the same way, of course, the Creator's approval can only really affect and change man's life when he 'realizes" it believingly, that is, when he also "accepts" it. (In general, knowledge really becomes a part of our vital stock only when we want to perceive it.)

Perhaps at this point we have to refer to a possible counter-position, such as Spinoza's terrifying conception that "God, strictly speaking, loves no one,"[13] in order to grasp the incredible alternative: that our own existence in fact testifies to nothing less than our being loved by the Creator. What this can specifically mean for man's relationship to the cosmos is movingly expressed by a remarkable, little known writer with somewhat old-fashioned solemnity, "But insomuch as God loves me because I am I, I am truly irreplaceable in the world."[14]

It seems clear to me that only through a conviction such as this can man achieve solid ground underfoot, within his own consciousness, as well. Presumably there exists something like a prime trustfulness by virtue of which one can live a "simple" life (in the Biblical sense of "single"[15]), that is, ultimately without complications (I am thinking of a character like the girl Chantal in George Bernanos' novel *Joy*). And if such prime trustfulness does exist, then it must consist in nothing less than the certainty of being so surpassingly, effectively and absolutely loved. I recall the words of a great student of human nature and a master of spirituality[16]: that simplicity, and he was referring here to the *simplicitas* of the New Testament, was at bottom nothing but "trusting to love." And with the peril of "loss of identity" so much discussed nowadays, it may be asked whether there is any other remedy for such dislocation other than this experience of existing because of being absolutely, irrevocably willed by the Creator. Granted, only faith can provide anyone with that feeling. But compared with the absolute stability of this foundation, the oft-praised "basis in solid facts" is truly quaking ground.

Within man, however, there is also a tendency to fend off the creative love that unasked and undeservedly has given him his own existence.[17] At bottom all love is undeserved. We can neither earn it nor promote it; it is always pure gift. It is even, as the motto of this book puts it, the "prime gift" that makes all other gifts possible. But there seems to be in man something like an aversion for receiving gifts. No one is wholly unfamiliar with the thought: I don't want anything for nothing! And this emotion comes uncannily close to the other: I don't want to be "loved," and certainly not for no reason! It was Nietzsche who made the acute remark that "people addicted to honor," that is people for whom their own importance is what chiefly matters, are "resistant to being loved."[18] And C. S. Lewis says that absolutely undeserved love is certainly what we need but not at all the kind of love we want. "We want to be loved for our cleverness, beauty, generosity, fairness, usefulness."[19] But the divine love of, as Dante puts it, the "First Lover" does not find anything of the kind to hand; as the possible object of His love nothing yet exists: *nihil.* But C. S. Lewis also speaks of the shocking fact of a (really or presumably or allegedly) "groundless" love of human beings for one another. This fact is so well known that people of ill will may even claim to love another person with a love they call Christian — because they know that this precisely will offend: "To say to one who expects a renewal of Affection, Friendship or Eros, 'I forgive you as a Christian,' is merely a way of continuing the quarrel. Those who say it are of course lying. But the thing would not be falsely said in order to wound unless, were it true, it would be wounding."[20]

But even if loving concern is innocently and gratefully experienced and accepted, whether this be the primal love of God or the love of a loving person, which is our principal theme here — the recipient is apt to feel something else besides encouragement and corroboration of his own existence. There is also, quite understandably, a sense of something akin to shame; being loved, one feels ashamed. It would seem that Plato first made mention of this truly curious fact. In the *Symposium*,[21] he has Phaedrus, the young man who is passionately stirred by the power of eros, speak at first of the fact that only lovers feel ashamed of doing anything shameful in each others' presence. But are they not ashamed because by loving each regards the other as better than he really *is*, objectively considered? The matter is somewhat more complicated than it seems at first sight.

First of all we must realize that the sense of shame we are dealing with here is a beneficial one; it has a "positive" aspect. For there also exists the contrary phenomenon of a destructive, "negative" sense of shame. This may also be bound up with the sense a person has that his real character by no means matches the opinion that people have (or had) of him. But because this shame is concerned principally with "exposure," such a feeling remains sterile; it obstructs the person affected instead of opening a path for him. In this connection we might well be reminded that the widespread practice of exposing a person to public ridicule, which has become standard fare for the "media" and is expected of them and greeted with amused interest, was once regarded in Occidental ethics as a specific form of injustice, the *peccatum derisionis*, a sin because it diminishes something that belongs to a man by right.[22]

On the other hand the "positive" and fruitful shaming that affects us in the experience of being loved, and probably only there, has something to do with the anticipatory nature of all true love. Granted, the lover is one who approves and affirms what is. Nevertheless, this affirmation of the beloved is in no way an undifferentiated approval of pure factuality. And the beloved is well aware that loving approval cannot be intended in this sense. That is the source of a discrepancy that repeatedly comes to light and that provides a very solid reason for feeling ashamed. Anyone who judges himself more or less without illusions knows perfectly well that what the lover tirelessly asserts simply isn't true: How wonderful that you exist; its glorious that you are; I love you! Perhaps others are saying bad things about you, but this person who loves you looks into your eyes and says, "I know you too well; you cannot possibly have ever done something like that!" In the Duc de La Rochefoucauld's *Maxims* there is the sardonic sentence: However people praise us, they are telling us nothing new. That is precisely the situation of lovers: Whatever the beloved is praised for comes as nothing new to the lover even though the beloved realizes that the praise is false and that he himself is far from glorious.

But that is only one side of the coin. The other side is that such praise of the beloved, although it may not correspond to actual facts, is not nceessarily simply false. In saying this we are, it must be granted, making several assumptions. Above all we are assuming that a real lover is speaking in a truly human fashion, that we are not hearing the casually phrased "mating calls" of mere sensuality. Furthermore, the lover must be able to perceive what the "purpose" of the other's being is and what he is meant by nature to attain. This in turn seems to confirm the old dictum that where love is an eye will open[23] so that the lover alone may succeed in perceiving the beloved's very purpose in being. In spite of everything that is, the beloved feels neither mistakenly lauded nor unappreciated or "misunderstood." Nicolai Hartmann in his *Ethics*[24] uses that word: "Instead of feeling misunderstood he (the beloved who has been thus praised) feels rather understood in a basic manner—and at the same time strongly urged to be as the other sees him."

Whether he does feel so strongly urged and whether, as Hartmann adds,[25] he will really be "pushed beyond himself"—although within rational limits—is a question dependent on another assumption: that the beloved for his part accepts this shaming and challenging love and responds lovingly to it. Suddenly he too now knows, perhaps for the first time, that he really could be and would be so "grand," that he could really achieve this special style of fairness, of bravery—*if* he actually carried out what he was made for and what the lover's eye has intuitively perceived through all the shells of empirical inadequacy.

Oddly enough — we must interject this here — being loved, or more strictly *wanting* to be loved, has come in for a good deal of scorn in recent times. It certainly does not enjoy a friendly press, and I think that this fact, complex as is everything that has to do with the subject of "love," conceals something hard to fathom, but rather important. Nietzsche[26] called wanting to be loved "the greatest of all presumptions." In psychoanalytical literature it is noted with disapproval[27] that most people see the problem of love as more one of being loved than of loving. Even Brecht comments that love is "the desire to give something, not to receive," and holds that the desire, or at any rate "the immoderate desire to be loved," has "little to do with genuine love."[28]

At first hearing all this sounds rather plausible; and to the extent that we keep our eye on infrahuman relations there is a good measure of truth in it. Plato, however, throws fresh light on the matter when he says that the lover is "more divine" than the beloved.[29] We might explicate the insight embodied in this phrase in a variety of ways, including the following: One would have to be God in order to be capable of loving without being dependent on being loved in return; it is a divine privilege always to be less the beloved than the lover; we (human beings) can never love God as intensely as He loves us; but above all: in his relationship to God it is quite appropriate for man to be loved more than to love. If we consider this last aspect, we may well wonder whether the general disparagement of wanting to be loved may not be a typically modern phenomenon, still another form of modern man's claim to equality with God.

Here, at any rate, is the point to remind ourselves of those thought-provoking phrases of Sigmund Freud, who speaks of the "part played by love in the genesis of conscience"[30] and defines "evil" as that "for which we are threatened with loss of love."[31] In all "guilt feelings," he argues, "fear of the loss of love"[32] is at work, the fear "that we will no longer be loved by this supreme power."[33] What "supreme power"? In his attempt to answer this question Freud misses the opportunity implicit in his magnificent beginning by defining that "supreme power" as the "mythical father of prehistoric times"[34] who, projected by way of the "Oedipus complex" into the collective and individual consciousness, engenders — as a "superego" — fear and guilt feelings. And in Freud's own view that, of course, is a wholly groundless, irrational reaction from which people ought to free themselves by bringing it to consciousness and "analyzing" it.

What Freud is calling for is clear: emancipation from dependence on the desire to be loved, which he views as founded on illusion, and therefore from the fear of losing love. Of course there is no denying what the researches of Sigmund Freud have compellingly demonstrated: that the conflict with the father (for instance) can be of enormous importance to psychic growth, to the formation of conscience, to the genesis of guilt feelings and also, sometimes, to the neurotically rampant growth of such guilt feelings. But can the Freudian explanation ultimately account for the psychological experience of *being* guilty? What if our existence itself really depended upon being wanted and being loved not by an imaginary prehistoric father figure, but by an extremely real, absolute Someone, by the Creator Himself? And what if at bottom being guilty ("sin") were really lack of being, resistance — to the extent that it is up to us — to that creative want and love of another in which, as we have already said, our existence literally consists? That, to be sure, is a totally different matter; and yet does not everything that Freud, with the penetration of genius, has to say about the part that love, including our own love, plays in the genesis of conscience and in the fear of losing love, suddenly acquire a remarkable pertinacity, within this framework?

When such thoughts are followed out, perhaps the familiar or even all too familiar Christian ideas of "a life pleasing to God" and of the "desire to please God" suddenly regain — or gain for the first time — something approaching the color of reality. As we have already said, in this realm words are constantly losing not only their sheen and their expressiveness but even their very meanings. The moment comes when they are nothing but sounding brass and can no longer be used seriously. (Consequently we must try to keep them alive and contemporaneous by special linguistic efforts!) Well then: "desire to please" — surely that must mean much the same as desire to be loved? The word *eudokein* (to be pleased with) occurs dozens of times in Biblical Greek; from the purely semantic point of view, "of all expressions for choosing" it conveys "most strongly the emotional tone of the chooser's love" according to the Kittel.[35] At any rate, it once again becomes evident that the fundamental aspects of existence (desire to be loved, loss of love, guilt, conscience, being "pleasing to God") may be found in close proximity. Within the same context we will also find the concept of "glory" (*gloria*) which the ancients unabashedly defined as *clara cum laude notitia*,[36] that is to say as "fame," as being publicly taken notice of and recognized by God Himself. At first it is actually a bit embarrassing, not to say shocking, to find the thing described so "naively." But the shock aims and hits deeper than we may think. For when we are asked to understand *gloria* as the supreme fulfillment of existence, as the "glory" of Eternal Life, we are expected to do two things. The first is to admit to ourselves that in our heart of hearts there is hardly anything we want so ardently as to be publicly "praised" and acknowledged. The second requirement is that we do not fall prey to the ideal of tight-lipped self-sufficiency, that gloomy resolve to take nothing as a gift, nor fall into the infantilism of needing constant confirmation. In other words, we are asked to adopt an attitude that might best be characterized as "childlikeness": a way of leading our life so that we actually achieve *gloria*, that is, the acknowledgment by the "First Lover," Who now "publicly," that is in the presence of all Creation, at once declares and sees to it that it is "glorious" to be the person we are.

IV

WE HAVE SEEN that loving concern, although it actually confirms the beloved in his existence, can also have a shaming element. This fact — which seems paradoxical only at first glance — indicates that love is not synonymous with undifferentiated approval of everything the beloved person thinks and does in real life. As a corollary, love is also not synonymous with the wish for the beloved to feel good always and in every situation, and for him to be spared experiencing pain or grief in all circumstances. "Mere 'kindness' which tolerates anything except [the beloved's] suffering"[1] has nothing to do with real love. St. Augustine expressed the same idea in a wide variety of phrases: "Love reprimands, ill will echoes";[2] "the friend speaks bitterly and loves, the disguised foe flatters and hates."[3] No lover can look on easily when he sees the one he loves preferring convenience to the good. Those who love young people cannot share the delight they seem to feel in (as it were) lightening their knapsacks and throwing away the basic rations they will eventually need when the going gets rough.

But, it might be argued, doesn't "loving someone" virtually mean: taking him as he really is "with all his weaknesses and faults"? After all, what else is it supposed to mean when someone says, "It's good that you are; it's wonderful that you exist"? In response I would first of all suggest that "exist" doesn't signify a purely static being-there, but something that is in process and that "continues." And of course the lover wishes it to continue *well*. But what about the weaknesses and faults? Aren't they inevitably a part of actual existence?

To answer this question at all adequately, several distinctions must first be considered — above all two. *First*, the distinction between, in brief, "weakness" and "guilt." "I'm a slow thinker and too quick to condemn; I have a tendency to fly off the handle — you'll have to take me the way I am!" This could, it seems to me, properly be said to one who claims to love us; this is not asking too much — even though, obviously, we can only be asking him to love us *in spite of* our weaknesses, not to love those weaknesses themselves. But compared with that, would it not be an entirely different matter if someone were to say, "I happen to be unjust, self-centered, dissolute (and so on) — and if you love me you'll have to take me the way I am"? Does not real love actually exclude that kind of acceptance and approval? Or, on the contrary, does real love perhaps only begin when faced with such faults?

At this point a *second* distinction proves essential, the distinction between two different ways of accepting something bad. One of these ways is proper to a lover; the other is not. I am referring to the distinction between excusing and forgiving.

As we all know, ordinary language does not draw too sharp a line between the areas of meaning covered by these two words. But their significance is fundamentally different. By "excusing" we mean discounting what is bad. We "let it be" although it is bad; we ignore the evil; we don't care; we are indifferent to it; we don't worry about it. Now there is very little if anything that a lover

40

should "excuse" in the above sense — whereas he can forgive the beloved *everything*. In fact forgiveness is one of the fundamental acts of love. But what specifically is meant by that? Certainly it does not mean "letting be" something bad, simply not regarding it as important — as though it were a mere oversight. We forgive something only if we regard it as distinctly bad, not if we ignore its negative aspect. And only forgiveness takes the other's personal dignity seriously; we are then not seeing him as a kind of apparatus which occasionally suffers functional disturbances and "breakdowns." Rather we are seeing him as a person who has *done* something.

On the other hand, forgiveness seems to assume that the other himself condemns ("repents") what he has done, and that he accepts the forgiveness. If we attempt to "forgive" someone although he stands by his wickedness and wants no forgiveness, we are in a very literal sense declaring him not of sound mind, not responsible for his actions. Moreover, strictly speaking we can only forgive and pardon something which has been done to ourselves. But as we have said, in all these matters ordinary language is not very precise and consistent, which is not to deny that it is expressive and valid.

Let us take, for example, a man living under conditions of despotism who has saved his life (or his job or his fortune) by an act of betrayal. What he betrayed may have been his own convictions or even a friend. What is the situation of the woman who loves this man with regard to excusing and forgiving? Specifically, all sorts of possibilities are conceivable. Perhaps this man is deceiving himself, glossing over his own failure, twisting his account of it to make himself seem guiltless, in any case "excusing" himself. To reinforce his efforts along these lines would of course smack more of complicity than real love. The true lover will not want the beloved to persist in such self-deception. He necessarily wishes him to free himself from it — which, of course, is not to say how this wish might be expressed or whether it would have to be expressed at all. But in any case, love cannot accept what is bad; love "excuses" *nothing*.

It is conceivable, too, that the man in question recognizes the inexcusability of his action, does not try to find any extenuation for it, and suffers because there is no longer a way to make up for it. His wife, although she lovingly sympathizes with his anguish, nevertheless could not wish him to be unaffected by what has happened. And although the act of injustice may not have involved her, she could grant him something like forgiveness precisely because he is suffering — although an outsider might scarcely be able to distinguish between her forgiveness and a mere excusing of his fault ("Let it be; think no more about it").

The fact remains that to love a person does not mean to wish him to live free of all burdens. It means, rather, to wish that everything associated with him may truly be good. From this point of view, the phrase about love's "inflexibility," which comes up so frequently in western moral philosophy, loses some of its strangeness. To be sure, it is hard to determine once and for all the boundary at which love's severity becomes loveless harshness, so that *in concreto* it can be almost impossible to distinguish excusing from forgiving and weakness from guilt.

Sometimes it is instructive to take an extreme example from which to read the answer to a difficult question. What it means to really love another person is such a question. Nor do we have to devise hypothetical cases for our purpose. A beloved person in the situation of a martyr is not at all inconceivable; we may think either of the mothers of young Christians facing the Roman proconsul or the wives of persecuted innocent men before the "people's courts" of modern dictatorships. Naturally these women do not want to lose their beloved sons or husbands;

naturally they are horrified at the thought of what is facing them; and of course they hope with all their hearts that their men may in some miraculous manner escape their fate and be restored to them. But could these women in all seriousness, out of love, wish that the person they love so dearly would accept the opportunity, or even the offer, to buy their freedom by an act of baseness? We are concerned now, it must be remembered, not with the "casuistical" discussion of moral standards, and certainly not with the question of how we ourselves might actually behave in such a situation. Our only point here is to bring to light by the exercise of our judgment on such an extreme case in what terms we desire everything to go perfectly well for a person close to us — which is to say, in what terms love operates.

I said "our judgment." For whether or not we are clearly conscious of it, our opinion of what love ultimately is reaches out far beyond the limits of our own direct experience. In the nature of things, everything we think about the world as a whole enters into this universal concept. And even those who declare human existence to be simply absurd, or who see it gloomily unfolding under the decrees of a blind fate, still have an inkling of that all-embracing love whose absence they lament or denounce. In the very manner of negation or mockery or perhaps even respect for the mystery of it all, there is present in the mind, whenever the world's evil is considered, some conception of *that* love which "turning moves the Sun and the other stars," as the last line of Dante's cosmic poem puts it. What I am saying is: an inevitable concomitant of thinking about love is some conception of what the love of God, the "First Lover," must be like.

And although, superficially considered, we would be quite pleased with a "senile benevolence who . . . liked to see the young people enjoying themselves"[4] we nevertheless know very well that the all-embracing love of Him

Who desires everything to go perfectly well for the world and man cannot be of this nature. Certainly our occasional timidity is not altogether incomprehensible. We may well wish sometimes that "God had designed for us a less glorious and less arduous destiny." But in our hearts we surely do not deceive ourselves; we know that in that case we are wishing "not for more love, but for less."[5] Incidentally, such a desire to escape the demands of love was so familiar to the thinkers of the past that they cited it among the seven "deadly sins" as *acedia*, that slothfulness of the heart to which Kierkegaard gave the name of "despair of weakness." By that he meant the despair of a man's not daring to be what he is. The upshot of all this indicates that our human understanding would never have found it so "unfathomable" that, as the mystics say, God's love can be "a thousand times sterner and harsher" than His justice.[6] We have been assuming that our concrete ideas about love (for a friend, for a sweetheart, for son and daughter) are partly shaped by an absolutely universal standard of "love" that is possibly hidden from "daylight consciousness." And if this is really true, it should not surprise us to find again in earthly human love the same stringent dispensation that combines affirmation and demand in a unity. Christendom's sacred book simply expresses what everyone has experienced: the bastards are pampered, but the sons are placed under discipline.[7]

Then what, ultimately and in terms of the whole, do we want when we truly love someone? The great tradition of European theology has answered this question: *ut in Deo sit*;[8] we wish that he may be in God. That is to be sure a very solemn response that voices the very limits of what we mean. But I venture to assert that it expresses the common view, even though, in a manner of speaking, it is a formal and solemn statement.

Now it is perfectly true that we cannot always speak this formally. Such excessive solemnity, such aiming at "the ultimate," as though something infinitely sublime and uncommon were constantly being asked of us, might even destroy love's essential reality among real people. It still remains true that all love directed toward a human being (it's good that you exist,") is a reflection of the Creator's creative love, by Whose "approval" all beings, including this beloved person, exist at all. Nevertheless, we do not have to show our love by consciously "re-enacting" the primal *creatio* in our own minds; we show it in the quite ordinary form of active helpfulness, in the friendliness of greetings and expressions of thanks, in a small word or even in a mere good-humored muttering — and, of course, in those infinitely difficult and yet wholly inconspicuous "acts" of which the New Testament[9] speaks: not being envious, not being boastful, not rejoicing at others' sorrows, bearing no grudges (and so on). On the other hand we might well be reminded now and again that even the scarcely noted ill humor in our daily life would, were its intention carried out to its ultimate conclusion, amount to a negation of the created world, to the desire that the other person might not exist at all. I am afraid that we cannot escape from these truly fearsome interrelationships by an act of "the despair of weakness," perhaps by looking at things from an exclusively psychological or sociological point of view. On the contrary, the horizon against which human love, just like hate, occurs is enormous.

Normally we accept the fact of our own existence unconsciously, as a matter of course, until this vital self-assurance is shaken by outward circumstances. But when that does happen it becomes clear that our acceptance of our own being, our assent to ourselves, our feeling at home in existence (and without self-affirmation, love for another person might not be possible at all) — this very courage for being is ultimately justifiable only by reference to the initial act of the Creator, Who brought us into existence as a reality that henceforth can never be removed from the world, that is not susceptible to "annihilation," and Who with absolute finality has declared it "good" that we exist. On what basis can anyone have such "courage for being"? Paul Tillich, who used this phrase as the title of one of his last books,[10] answers the question himself: "We consciously affirm that we *are* affirmed."[11]

But does not all that has been said about the severity and the challenge of love comport rather with the image of a moralistic schoolmaster than with that of a lover? Does not the wish that another person's situation may be "entirely good" seem a long way off from being real love? Can we not sincerely wish someone "all the best" — as we repeatedly do in leavetakings or in the complimentary closes of letters — without loving him? In fact, is there not an element of aloofness in this phrase, and do we not use it deliberately to keep him at a distance? All these objections, which I perfectly well understand, might be summed up in the one question: Does "good will," "benevolence," "wishing well," constitute the essence of love?

I would answer this question in three ways. *First*, it is certainly no small thing for a person to feel sincere good will toward another. *Second*, authentic love certainly requires that one person wish another well, or rather "the" good. *Third*, good will is not in itself enough to constitute what we mean by love.

Concerning this last point we must mention a remarkable correction that Thomas Aquinas introduces into the famous Aristotelian definition which runs, in the Latin translation he cites: *amare est velle alicui bonum*,[12] to love means to wish someone the good. In the more complete text of Aristotle's *Rhetoric* it goes: "To love means to wish another everything we think good, and moreover for the other's sake, not for our own."[13] This clear and refined definition has rightly been repeated many times in classical treatises on the great subject of "love." Cicero, too, can find nothing better to say.[14] Thomas Aquinas, however, as we have said, explicitly takes up this point when he asks, "Is loving (*amare*) insofar as it is an act of *caritas* the same as wishing well (*benevolentia*)?"[15] He is speaking here, it must be realized, not of the *passio amoris*, not of the primarily sensual rapture kindled by the sight of the beloved, but of mental and spiritual love which goes beyond mere fascination: *caritas*. Thomas asserts, then, that to equate *caritas* with mere well-wishing, *benevolentia*,[16] is to define it inadequately. Granted, no love can exist without such benevolence, but benevolence is patently something quite different from love.

But a qualification seems ready to hand. Of course well-wishing is not enough; the wish must be translated into doing good for someone. But that is not where Thomas takes issue with Aristotle's definition. And in fact, to repeat the words of Karl Jaspers, it is perfectly possible for there to be "charity without love," a *doing* good which lacks something decisive to make it love. In her moving book *On Death and Dying*, in which the Swiss-American physician Elizabeth Kübler-Ross describes her experiences with dying persons,[17] she points out that in modern hospitals the moribund patient is an object of great medical interest, and incidentally also of enormous financial investments ("He will get a dozen people around the clock, all busily preoccupied with his heart rate, pulse, electrocardiogram . . . his secretions or excretions"[18]), but that the patient will not succeed, no matter how much he insists, in persuading a single one of these busy people to pause for a minute and listen to a question, let alone answer it. Those in attendance are very much concerned with physiological processes, but not with the patient himself as a human being. If they paused, it is said, they might lose precious time that could be better spent saving the patient's life. Probably that is true, and we should try not to be too facile about criticizing anyone. But what the patient misses is being regarded as a person. Such concern for the human being himself need not necessarily be "love"; but it would be a first step toward love.

This is precisely what Thomas Aquinas implies when he says that something is missing to make well-wishing (and doing-good) into real love. He calls the missing element the *unio affectus*,[19] volition directed toward the other person, the wish to be with him, to be united with him, in fact to identify with him. When the true lover says, "It's good that you exist," he wants to be one with the person he loves.

This once again confirms, from another angle, that love's act of approval is not intended as a mere verification; rather, it is an impulse of the will that takes the person of the other as its partner and is involved in the other himself, an act of affirmation, or as Alexander Pfänder somewhat dramatically phrases it, "a momentary, centrifugal striking out in the direction of the beloved person."[20]

But now this coin also has to be turned over once more so that we may see its reverse. "How wonderful that you exist" — certainly this impulse has more of an "impact" than a mere observation. Yet it obviously presupposes observation and verification! A necessary assumption is that *before* we have that impulse of the will we find it "good" and "wonderful" that this other, this beloved person, exists. In other words, we must previously have *perceived* that the other's existence, and the other himself, is something good and wonderful. Without such a preceding experience, no impulse of the will can exist in any meaningful way. That is, without such experience we cannot love at all, nothing and no one. First of all, what is lovable must have revealed itself to our eyes, to our sensuous as well as mental faculty of perception: *visio est quaedam causa amoris*,[21] seeing is a kind of cause of love.

However, to find lovable and to love are two different matters. And the step from the one to the other need not necessarily be taken. If it is actually taken, that happens out of the spontaneity of volition; or to say it another way: out of freedom. At any rate love is in no way a logical conclusion which we can be compelled to draw. The situation is similar to the case of belief: the step from finding somebody trustworthy to really believing him is likewise nothing that can be determined by reasons, no matter how "compelling." "To believe someone" and "to love someone" — these are by their nature spontaneous acts in which, if we do not choose to call them simply "free," freedom certainly plays a part. Incidentally, that is the reason why both acts are peculiarly opaque and akin to mysteries. And yet in order for these spontaneous and opaque acts, whether belief or love, to be performed at all, there remains an indispensable prerequisite: the perception that someone is credible or lovable. We must have experienced and "seen" that the other person, as well as his existence in this world, really is good and wonderful; that is the precondition for the impulse of will which says, "It's good that you exist!"

But I do not mean to elaborate anything resembling an "epistemology of love." What concerns me is the previous step. Granted, it is true that one cannot love until he has seen and understood. But understanding is vain if it fails to grasp a reality — if, that is, it is wrong. In other words, if independently of our seeing, perceiving and thinking it is not *really* "good" that the beloved person exists, then all this approval is a deception, mistake, wishful thinking, a delusion. And then all love is an illusionary play of blind instinctual impulses, a trick of nature, as Schopenhauer[22] says, an unreal mirage and a self-deception striking at the heart of the "Lover's" own being.

"How good that you exist!" — well yes, but must we not in some way be able to feel certain that it really is "good"? But on the basis of what can we feel certain of that? How do we know such a thing?

49

As a tentative answer I would suggest that for such a demanding process of ascertainment we would have to expect the whole person with all his powers of comprehension to be the organ of perception, and that each of his "reflectors" must be "operative" — from the direct experience of the senses to the intellectual powers of thought and seeing and all the way to the insight, which only faith can bestow, into the nature of the universe and man as creations. And there are many indications that when the senses no longer observe beauty and the intellect can no longer detect any meaning or value, what ultimately sustains love and remains believable as its real justification is the conviction that everything existing in the universe is *creatura*, creatively willed, affirmed, loved by the Creator and for that reason is really — in the most radical sense that the word "really" can possibly have — *really* good and therefore susceptible to, but also worthy of, being loved by us.

But isn't it clear that this exclamation, "It's good that this exists; how wonderful that you are," by its very nature does *not* refer to "everybody," let alone the whole of Creation? In the ordinary course of events doesn't it refer to a single "chosen" being?

In America the attempt has been made to trace the innumerable, widely different interpretations of the phenomenon of love that are to be found in the tradition of occidental thought from Plato to psychoanalysis, to compare and discuss them, and to reduce them to a relatively comprehensible number of fundamental ideas. In the book[23] that sums up the results, a very few characteristics, to be numbered on the fingers of one hand, are found to recur in all characterizations of love. Among these is preference; "to be loved . . . is normally to be singled out."[24] Sigmund Freud regards this aspect of the phenomenon as so crucial that he specifically considers it an argument against the ideal of a universal human love. Incidentally, he mentions two such arguments; we shall come to the second in due time. He formulates the first reservation as follows, "A love that is not selective seems to us to forfeit part of its value by doing the object an injustice."[25] At first sight it seems as if this could scarcely be controverted. But a second glance shows us the matter in a somewhat different light. For if we look to the well-documented experience of great lovers we learn that precisely this intensity of love turned toward a single partner seems to place the lover at a vantage point from which he realises for the first time the goodness and lovableness of all people, in fact of all living beings. This exceptional love offered to one single person who takes precedence over all others, this love that fills us so utterly that it would seem no room was left for any other love — this very love that is so restrictive evidently makes possible a universality of affirmation that prompts the lover to say, "How wonderful that all this exists!" "A heart that loves one person cannot hate anyone" — that is a Goethean dictum.[26] Dante says precisely the same thing in regard to Beatrice: When she appeared "no foe existed for me any more."[27]

I would not be disconcerted if someone were to say at this point: All very well, those are the statements of poets and mean nothing in regard to "concrete reality" (nor are they even meant to).* The authentic poet, of course, is not one who naively or intentionally — like the sophist[28] — embodies any wishful thinking that comes his way. The poet, to be sure, does not simply describe everyman's empirical reality; but he brings to consciousness something that this everyman in his better moments can recognize as what he had all along dimly sensed, what at

---

*We have here the familiar translation problem of *Dichter* and *Dichtung*. "Poet" is here used in the wider sense of creative writer, and "poetry" of imaginative writing.

bottom he has long known and can corroborate. With the aid of the poet's imagination we suddenly "know": Ah yes, things could happen this way in the world of men if — of course *not* "if men were all angels," but if by a happy dispensation we were enabled to act out our true humanity, as happens in the case of love. It is no accident that from time immemorial poetry has glorified love!

In saying this we must be clear about two distinct matters. On the one hand such universal human love cannot accomplish anything practical in the world; man's historical predicaments cannot be solved by love. But on the other hand — as we likewise know very well — ideal universal love isn't simply an unrealistic fantasy. Rather, it is an innate potentiality reminiscent as it were, of paradise which is revealed for a moment solely in the exceptional figures of great lovers. (Freud speaks of St. Francis of Assisi.)

The following sentence similarly rests upon the conviction of the *universal* goodness of all things by reason of their creation: "Good without evil can exist, evil without good cannot."[29] We cannot simply confirm such a proposition on the basis of our everyday experience; and yet we know that it is fundamentally true, that it is right.

All this has nothing whatsoever to do with any sort of naive Pollyannaism. It is not to be forgotten that love also makes hate possible; one who cannot love also cannot hate. For the time being I shall leave out of consideration Catullus's famous couplet, *Odi et amo* ("I hate and love and if you ask me why, I have no answer, but I discern, can feel, my senses rooted in eternal torture"[30]); involved in that are the peculiarities of erotic love, which we shall not discuss just yet. I am referring now to hatred for everything that threatens to corrupt those whom we love; this is the hatred that accompanies love.

Jealousy is also quite close to our theme. But it must be remembered that there are two kinds of jealousy.[31] One

kind is the jealousy of the covetous who want to keep
thing or someone for themselves alone, but are not sec
their possession. Such jealousy in fact runs contrary
idea of the universality of love. But it is quite another
ter to be jealous not "of" someone who is to be exc
but "for" someone (or something), to feel angry, irrec
able hostility toward everything (and to feel it sel
rather than selfishly) that might possibly impugn th
loved subject. The English word "jealousy" is derived
the Latin *zelus*, which is used in that sense in the P
(Ps 69, 9): "Zeal for thy house has consumed me."
disciples of Jesus remember this passage when He
the money-changers out of the temple (Jn 2, 17).
hard to say against what and whom that fierce antag
is directed. But in any case we had better dismis
thought that the call for universal love imposes a
annaish view of the real world!

Sigmund Freud, I said, mentions two objections
ideal of universal human love. His second is: "Al
are not lovable."[32] At first this statement strikes
more or less a commonplace, something we all di
every day. But as soon as we consider it in the li
principle, as soon as we radicalize it, so to spea
realize what a monstrous assertion it is. For is i
tantamount to saying that there are people in rega
whom it would be impossible, and unjustifiable for a
to say, "It's good that you exist?" But who could po
have the right even to think such a thought seriousl

Probably two matters must be more closely scrut
here. The first has already been mentioned briefly:
degrees of approbation exist, and that they are quite
mate. Alongside the superlative of passionate prais
the beloved there are also varieties of less passionat
no less sincere and dependable affirmation. For exa
anyone who seriously carried out what in colloquial s
is called "live and let live" would not be altogether r

from that "making be" which we have defined as one of the specific achievements of love. And even mere "acceptance" can be an extremely important matter, as an expression of affirmation. The point should be made, by the way, that the statements by poets cited above do not refer to any outpouring of universal brotherhood. They merely say, though with emphatic clarity, that "great" love enables a person to be nobody's enemy; great love keeps anyone from saying with regard to someone else, "You ought not to exist."

Probably even Sigmund Freud's remark that all men are not lovable was scarcely intended in any such drastic sense as we can take it in, when we regard it in purely abstract terms. Nevertheless, it brings us back to the question raised earlier: On what basis is man prohibited (and, psychologically speaking, what could stop him?) from saying in all seriousness of another person: He ought not to exist. Not: I wish he weren't here; and not: I wish he were dead; but: God ought not to have created him. It is this last and most radical formulation that once again presents the only cogent "reason" which could make it impossible for us to wish the non-existence of a single created being or thing, were it only an atom of the material universe.

The second point that Sigmund Freud's comment forces us to consider is that "to call a person lovable or not lovable" can mean something entirely different from affirming or negating his existence. And in everyday language it may be that this other meaning is always the one intended, to wit, positive or negative estimation of a person's "qualities." The helpful neighbor is lovable; so are the pleasant coworker, the amusing companion, the fair fellow-sportsman, the elegant dancing partner — and so on. A French writer proposes that in such cases we ought not to speak of "love" but of sympathy.[33] But if we ignore the question of terminology for the time being — a question

that could give rise to endless disputes — we must at any rate concede that two different modes of concern for another person are involved. In the one case the affirmation is directed primarily to his existence, in the other case to his *essentia*, to the way he is. In the literature these two aspects are sometimes sharply opposed to one another; in fact each is used to counter the other. Thus it has been said that the true lover does not look to "qualities" at all, but only to the person.[34] Elsewhere it is even argued that according to experience "the attempt to love a person for his or her qualities — be they spiritual or physical, intellectual or temperamental — deteriorates into a kind of prostitution in which the person is used and valued for what he does and has. Relationships based on the mutual admiration of qualities end in disillusion and often in bitterness."[35]

At first hearing such a formulation sounds odd and disturbing. It acquires somewhat more plausibility when we supplement it by a remark along the same lines by Emil Brunner. Brunner says, "The formula for love is *not*: I love you because you are *thus* — and we might add: *as long as* you are thus."[36] It is precisely this addition that suddenly illuminates the matter; for it is evident to everyone that if a love ends the moment certain of the partner's qualities (beauty, youth, success) vanish, it never existed from the first. The test question, once again, is *not*. Do you find the other person likable, capable, "nice"? Rather, the question is: Are you glad for his existence, or do you have anything against it; can you honestly say, "It's good that he exists?"

But of course, on the other hand, existence and the qualities of the existing person cannot be separated; there is no such thing as *existentia* without *essentia*. Even while the lover beholds the beloved[37] he naturally sees both; he cannot ignore the qualitative aspect, the rough sketch that the other person is destined to refine. This nature as a sketch, this perception of what the beloved was "really" intended to become, may be perceptible only to the lover's prophetic eye, as we have already said. And perhaps what also happens is that love, when it is taking its very first step, is kindled by the beloved's *essentia*. In other words, incipient love may after all be attracted by "qualities" (beauty, charm, flashing intelligence). But when it has become real love it will then penetrate to the core of the person who stands behind these qualities and who "has" them, to the true subject of that unimaginable act that we call existing, to the beloved's innermost self, which *remains* even when the lovable qualities long since have vanished, those same qualities that once upon a time, far back at the beginning, may have approximated a "reason" for love.

In this light the "formula" for true love that Emil Brunner likewise proposes, "I love you because you exist," seems to me to be a quite unrealistic construction. No lover has ever said anything like that. He says, "It's good that you exist." But he has nothing to do with becauses and reasons. As I say, there may have been reasons in the incipient stages; but after love has developed, it no longer has need of them.

V

IT's GOOD THAT you exist" — good for whom? So far we
have not asked this question; but it is easy to see that it
strikes to the heart of the matter. Obviously it makes a
decisive difference whether we think it good for *our sake*
that the other person exists (because we need him), or for
his sake (because we want him to be happy and to arrive
at the fulfillment intended for him). But if we find it
good for *our sake* — can it be said that we love the other
person?

In regard to love for the good things of this life, there
is no problem at all. Of course we love wine (for example)
for our own sakes. "It would surely be ridiculous," says
Aristotle, "to wish for the good of wine (that is, to love
it for its own sake); if one wishes it at all, it is that the
wine may keep, so that we can have it for ourselves."[1] It
has rightly been said, however, that it is possible for us to
esteem beloved things in an entirely disinterested fashion
and simply to rejoice "that such a thing exists" — like
this choice burgundy or these rare stones or fine jewelry.[2]
Even in the narrower area of human sensuality such an
aloofness from mere desire is conceivable. Thomas Aquinas
mentioned as something distinctively human the ability to

experience sensual and sensuous concord, *convenientia sensibilium*, without the intervention of desire;[3] animals, he points out, observe only the possible object for eating and coupling, whereas man, by disciplining his desires, is alone capable of enjoying sensuous beauty such as that of the human body *as* beauty.[4] But in digressing thus we have unexpectedly come back to the relationships of men to men. At any rate, what we want to remember is that there is nothing untoward in our loving things for our own sakes, in saying, "It's good that that exists — good for us!"

The difficulty begins when we love another person for our own sake. But that must be put more precisely. It is quite clear that the relationship of the sexes can include forms of sheer selfish use and abuse, as well as sexual subservience, that have nothing to do with love among men. St. Augustine has expressed the matter as follows, "It is not permissible to love people in the same way as one hears gourmets say: I love carp."[5] There really is no serious disput on this score. The real question, the one on which opinions divide, runs as follows: Whenever some-one says, "It's good that you exist, good for me, because I cannot be happy without you," is this always a distortion of love? Is it unworthy for anyone, or at least any *Christian*, to love in such a fashion? Is it part of the essence of truly human love for the lover to want absolutely nothing for himself, neither joy nor happiness nor any other en-richment of his vital store? Is selflessness simply one of the essential characteristics of all human love that deserves the name? But on the other hand, is not the longing for fulfilled existence actually and legitimately the root of all love? And is, in general, man capable of such absolute altruism that he would wish not to be happy?

Here it becomes apparent that in discussing the subject of "love," we must also consider the conception we have of man. It is always involved. In Plato's famous dialogue on this subject, after biology, psychology and sociology have put in their word, Aristophanes arises to say: No one understands anything about love who has not considered the nature of man and what has befallen it, the *pathémata anthrópou*; and then he tells the myth of man's original perfection and his guilty loss of it.[6] The aforementioned American attempt to simplify and catalogue the multitude of theories of love likewise arrives at the same intermediate result: "How love is understood follows from how human nature is understood."[7]

The phrase "human nature" in such contexts should probably be taken more literally than is generally done. Strictly speaking, the problem at issue is not so much what kind of being man is, but rather what he is "by nature." What is the character of and what happens with what man possesses and brings into the world with him by birth (*natura* comes from *nasci*, to be born)? We need only formulate this in such a bold fashion to find ourselves inevitably drifting, as happened to Plato also, into the realm of theology, and probably into highly controversial theology at that. As has been said, here opinions divide!

C. S. Lewis relates that when he began to write his book about love, which was published in 1960, he had intended pretty much without a qualm to sing the praises of pure, selfless, giving love, what he called "gift-love," and to speak more or less deprecatorily of craving, desirous "need-love."[8] But then he changed his mind. "The reality is more complicated than I supposed."[9] That such an attitude is assumed, before reflection, reveals to what extent the collective consciousness and the atmosphere of thought, especially of Christian thought concerning love, has already been moulded by a particular conception. We must now elaborate somewhat on that conception.

What is involved, to anticipate, is the antithesis of *eros* and *agape*. Here eros does not stand primarily for love between the sexes, but for all demanding and needing love. Thus it appears to be diametrically opposed to that love which alone seems proper to the Christian, for which reason it has undergone an explicit and, we must say, a fateful defamation. The phraseology may differ somewhat (*Eros and Caritas, Eros and Agape, Eros and Love* are the titles of three books published in the thirties[10]) — but the common element is always the deprecation of eros. The authors of those three books are all theologians,[11] and their theses are based upon a particular interpretation of the sacred tradition, chiefly of the New Testament. Inevitably, however, they imply a more universal, pretheological conception of man; and that is of concern to everyone who reflects upon the life of man.

The most radical and, in terms of intellectual history, the most provocative formulation of the thesis of "eros and agape" may be found in the two-volume book by that title, the work of the Swedish theologian Anders Nygren.[12] This book has had almost incalculable influence, although of course it iself may well spring from an idea that has probably always been present in Christendom as a subterranean current. For the moment I shall attempt here to present Nygren's thesis in a necessarily summary fashion, beginning with his characterization of the two basic concepts.

Agape, "the original basic conception of Christianity,"[13] "above all others the basic Christian motif,"[14] signifies primarily an almost entirely unselfish love, a yielding rather than self-assertive love, the love that does not seek to win life but dares to lose it.[15] Agape "has nothing to do with desire or lust";[16] it "fundamentally excludes everything that implies self-love."[17] Here Nygren cites Martin Luther's: *Est enim diligere seipsum odisse*,[18] to love means to hate oneself. Of course that is not to be taken altogether literally. Nevertheless, agape stands in irreconcilable opposition "to all eudemonistically founded action,"[19] that is to say, to all motivation based on the desire for happiness, let alone "for reward."[20] At bottom there is no "motive" at all for agape; rather, it is explicitly "unmotivated."[21] Motivation, in the sense that something else is "moving" it, would in fact signify a kind of dependence on that something else; but agape "needs nothing at all from outside to set it in motion."[22] It is therefore "indifferent"[23] to predetermined values. In conclusion Nygren uses the word "spontaneity"[24] to define the decisive characteristic, the "upwelling"[25] nature of agape. With similar significance he also speaks of its "sovereignty"[26] and its "creative" character,[27] since it creates values instead of assuming them.[28]

Eros is, point by point, the counterpoise to agape. It is neither creative nor spontaneous, because it is essentially determined by its object, by the pre-existing goodness and beauty whose presence is first discovered and thereupon loved.[29] Primarily, of course, eros is "love of a desirous, egocentric kind."[30] "The starting point is human need, the goal is the satisfaction of this need."[31] "Eros is fundamentally self-love,"[32] even in its most sublime form, even when it is conceived as a "way of man toward the divine."[33] Explicitly included in this condemnation is St. Augustine's well-known phrase[34] that man's heart is restless until it reposes in God. Here, Nygren argues, it becomes apparent that Augustine is fully under the influence of Plato's doctrine of eros, which has nothing to do with the Christian idea of love.[35] "No way, not that of sublimation either, leads from eros to agape."[36]

Yet in Nygren's opinion this very attempt at a "sublimation of desirous love or self-love into pure divine love"[37] began very early, by the incorporation of Platonic, which means pagan, ideas into Christian philosophy. As an example of this Nygren mentions Gregory of Nyssa[38] who speaks of the soul's rising to God, of the ladder to heaven, of the upleaping flame and the wings of the soul. This poor compromise, Nygren continues, which tries to unite incompatibles, was first developed into a system by St. Augustine — the systematization resulting in the *"caritas* synthesis."[39] But it remained for Thomas Aquinas to carry the error to its logical conclusion. To be sure, Thomas reduced everything in Christianity to love, but everything in love to self-love.[40] This wrongheaded harmonization of eros and agape by Thomas Aquinas falsified the original Christian intention, with the consequence that "the place where Christian agape-love . . . might have found a refuge has completely and finally vanished."[41]

Nygren goes on to interpret the end of the Middle Ages and the beginning of modern times as a shattering of that objectively unjustifiable "synthesis." On the one hand it was smashed by Renaissance man's philosophy of life, which made an absolute of eros; on the other hand by Martin Luther, who restored the idea of agape in its unadulterated purity.[42] Nygren sees Luther's achievement as primarily one of destruction; and the phrases he uses are unusual in their vehemence. "Luther smashed to pieces" that false synthesis;[43] he "regarded it as his principal task to annihilate the classical Catholic idea of love, the *caritas* synthesis";[44] he was "the destroyer of the Catholic view of love built up essentially on the eros factor."[45] That is, assuredly, forthright and energetic language, which does not try to blur antitheses. The same may be said for Nygren's terse conclusion: *"On the one hand* — in Catholicism — desirous love is the bond that holds everything together . . . *On the other hand* — in Luther — we are dealing with the religion and the ethos of agape."[46]

In this summary account, the wealth of argument and historical evidence that Nygren presents is, of course, barely suggested. Reading his book left me much perplexed — especially concerning the kind of love to be demanded of and expected of human beings. I found I simply could not accept the whole idea. Certainly this disparagement of eros, propounded with such force and held up as the only Christian view, has penetrated the general consciousness outside as well as inside Christendom. And I ask myself whether it may not be partly responsible for the disesteem directed against Christianity nowadays, precisely on the grounds of what Nature really or supposedly accords to man as his due in the realm of eros.

It is not as if Nygren's thesis, especially its depreciation of needful, demanding love, represents only one special opinion on the radical fringe. I must add a word about that. For me it was a saddening surprise to find Nygren seconded by a theologian of the rank of Karl Barth, of whom Hans Urs von Balthasar rightly says that we must "probably go back to St. Thomas to find again such freedom from all tension and narrowness."[47] In fact Karl Barth in his doctrine of the Creation speaks with magnificently realistic candor of erotic love between man and woman, of the joys to be found in it, of mutual liking and deciding in favor of one another. He regards the moralistic rigor of Calvin, who "had his wife picked out by close acquaintances," as definitely not worth imitating. As for the German Reformer, he comments, "Let us hope Luther was not being entirely serious when he once remarked that he had married Katharina von Bora in order to deliver a blow to the papacy."[48] Here, evidently, clearly "erotic" love, kindling in the personal encounters of human beings with real bodies and by no means "unmotivated," is named by name and frankly defended. But when in his doctrine on Redemption the same Karl Barth, discusses "the problem of Christian love," and formally addresses the subject of "eros and agape,"[49] he comes up with almost the same negative evaluation of eros as Nygren. Who influenced whom here (Barth is four years older than Nygren), and whether there is any dependence at all, seems to me of no importance. Still and all, in spite of his occasional rather sharp criticism of Nygren,[50] we find Karl Barth also discussing the "medieval" "*caritas* synthesis," and making the point that the opposition between "biblical agape" and "classical or Hellenistic eros" has remained "not outrightly unrecognizable but at this distance not unequivocally recognizable."[51]

As we can see from this phraseology, Barth is not so doctrinaire as Nygren. Swiss realist that he is, Barth is simply too close to an understanding of the average Christian's ordinary life ("As long as there are loving people they will, whether Christians or not, always live within the pattern of eros";[52] there is "certainly no Christian who in more refined or cruder form (and probably in both) does not also 'love' this way, by the standard of this entirely different mode of love,"[53] that is, the mode of eros). Nevertheless Karl Barth again and again expresses his fundamentally negative evaluation of eros. For him, too, eros as "self-love,"[54] as a "coarser or finer appetite,"[55] is "the diametrical opposite of Christian love."[56] "Every moment of tolerance" for eros-love "would be a decidedly un-Christian moment."[57] And even "the contention that it is a kind of preliminary stage of Christian love"[58] is insupportable. "The whole strangeness of Christianity within the world around it becomes apparent in the divorce which also runs through the individual Christian — of Christian love from that other love."[59]

Something else is revealed in this last, very fundamental sentence, just as we conjectured from the start. It is that in all this talk about love in general and eros in particular a conception of the nature of man is implicit, of what we might call man's "pre-Christian" nature, as given to him when he was created. Is it really something "strange," really "divorced" from Christianity? Or is it possibly the very ground without which the Christian element, the supernatural, grace (or whatever else we may wish to call this new dimension) could not take root and thrive?

But above all: if the natural man and that which he is and possesses by virtue of his creation has nothing to do with agape — then who, strictly speaking, is the subject of it? Who is really the lover here? Anders Nygren gives us a clear answer to this question. He gives it by interpreting a dictum of Martin Luther's. Luther's dictum runs as follows: "Whoso remaineth in love . . . is no longer a mere man, but a god." Nygren's interpretation is: that means that "the real subject of Christian love is not man, but God himself." And what about man? He is only "the conduit, the channel that conducts God's love."[60]

The answer is, as we have said, clear enough; but it also exposes the profoundly dubious nature, in fact the inherent impossibility, of the entire conception. For on the one hand agape, initially meaning not God's own love but the only kind of love that is proper for the Christian and requisite of him, is described as something independently sovereign in its absolute selflessness. It is characterised as spontaneous, overflowing, creative. It is, among Nygren's followers, hailed in the wildest terms: "The love that loves without reason and receives nothing";[61] " a love that is prepared to receive nothing at all, but only to give."[62] That is, on the one hand it imposes a tremendous demand upon man, but also represents a tremendous demand by man. But on the other hand, when we ask the question: who is the subject that is supposed to perform such a love, the answer we are given is startling, for this same man is suddenly no longer involved. He himself is not the one who loves! On his side there is not only no creative sovereignty; there is absolutely nothing at all!

Before we go into the details of the argument, we had best present our own thesis without more ado. We contest both the nothingness and the sovereignty — and in so doing we are clearly in accord with the great tradition of thought in the Christian West (from Augustine through

65

Thomas Aquinas to Francis de Sales, Leibnitz and C. S. Lewis, the great lay theologian of the present day). We are not in the least "nothing"; rather we are *creatura* and thereby have an existence that is our own — God-given, certainly, but for that very reason given to us to be truly our own. At the same time man, because of this same creatureliness, is by nature a totally needful being; he is himself "one vast need,"[63] a thirst that must be quenched, "the hungry being pure and simple."[64] And both aspects, our being somebody and our needfulness, come most plainly of all to light when we love.

VI

ANDERS NYGREN IS concerned with the many ramifications and implications of man's "nothingness" and the insignificance of everything that man as a physical being brings with him into the world by nature and birth, which is to say, by virtue of his having been created. Because this is strictly speaking a theological subject, we will not go into it too deeply here. Nygren is also concerned with Plato's question about "man's nature and what has happened to it." That question involves the primal sin committed in inconceivably ancient times but whose effects still continue into the present. The important point here is how that sin has affected human nature and its power to love. The extent to which Nygren deals with these questions is indicated, for example, by his mentioning the Manichaean-Gnostic sectarian Marcion as one of the ancestors of his own doctrine of agape. The church clearly and finally parted ways with Marcion in the second century. Marcion, says Nygren,[1] was one of the first advocates of the idea of agape. Marcion claimed that the Christian God "had nothing to do with the Creation." Nygren takes up this argument and carries it further, contending that "the absolutely unmotivated" aspect of agape becomes understandable only upon the basis of such a denial "of all connection between creation and redemption."

The logic of all this seems sound, yet it brings to light once more, in almost alarming fashion, the whole dubiousness of Nygren's conception. But as we have said, this is all in the realm of pure theology that is, a specific interpretation of sacred tradition and revelation. We, on the other hand, who wish to consider the question from the viewpoint of philosophy can scarcely contribute anything on our own. What we can do, however, and should do, is to state our own premises, or more precisely, what we believe or do not believe in regard to this matter. In so doing we are not ourselves engaging in theology, although we refer to and appeal to, perhaps inevitably, a theology we consider legitimate. For my part I have to cite what the great tradition of Christendom has held down to the present day: namely, that inherent in the concept of being created is the proposition that the *creatura* cannot itself dispose of the existence it possesses; that, therefore, even if it wanted to it could neither change nor, certainly, destroy its own nature. Just because man had been summoned into existence by the absolutely creative power of God, he remains — possibly even *malgré liu-meme* — what he is by virtue of his creation: a personal self and an individual. And it is this individual, man himself, who in love turns to another individual and says, "It's good that you exist!" In turning to another person with love man is *not* a "channel" and "conduit." Then if ever he is truly subject and person. And in "supernatural" love also, whether it is called *caritas* or "agape," and although it draws its force from "grace" — in that kind of love, too, the lovers are we ourselves.

The second thing we know is knowledge gained far more directly, on the basis of our own inner experience: that our love is anything but "sovereign." Above all, moreover, it never creates "values" or makes anything or anyone lovable. Rather the same rationale is basic to it as that from which all human activities derive their character of being grounded in the real: that Being comes first, and then Truth, and finally Goodness. Applied to our theme, what this means is: What comes first is the actual existence of lovability, independently presented to us. Then this existence must enter into our experience. And only then, hence anything but "unmotivatedly" and "without reason," do we say in confirming love, "It's good that this exists!"

That precisely is the meaning of a sentence of Thomas Aquinas which Nygren singles out for disapproving and almost indignant comment. That Thomas Aquinas "did not shrink" from writing it down, proves, to Nygren, that he reduced "everything in love to self-love"[2] and that, therefore, he could no longer open his mind at all to the original concept of pure agape. The sentence runs: "Assuming the impossible case that God were not really a good for man, there would be no reason for man to love."[3] What does this mean? Nothing less than that the emotion "It's good that you exist" has justification solely in the actual goodness of the beloved; that this is its basis in reality; and that this order of things applies not only to our love for material goods and our fellow men, but likewise to our love for God, and still applies in the Eternal Life.[4]

How in the world could our love for God be "groundless" and "unmotivated," let alone "sovereign"? It would indeed be "a bold and silly creature that came before its Creator with the boast, 'I'm no beggar. I love you disinterestedly.'"[5] Our love of God cannot help being largely if not entirely need-love.[6] Is it consequently eros, that is, basically self-love? If we do not forget that self-love is not necessarily "selfish" and that disinterested self-preservation[7] can exist, the answer to this question can only be: Yes.

But such need-love, whose goal is its own fulfillment, is also the nucleus and the beginning in all our loving. It is simply the elemental dynamics of our being itself, set in motion by the act that created us. Hence it is fundamentally impossible for us to control it, let alone to annul it. It is the "yes" that we ourselves *are* before we are consciously able to say "yes" (or even "no"). Here Augustine's idea, constantly reiterated in many forms throughout his entire work, acquires a perhaps unexpectedly precise meaning: *Pondus meum amor meus*,[8] my love is my weight; where it goes I go. We can no more govern this primal impulse, which affects all our conscious decisions, than we or any other being can have dominion over our own natures.[9] And, once again, it is inevitable and incontestable that this natural urge for fulfilment and completion is basically *self-love*. "Angels like men by nature strive for their own good and their own perfection; and this means loving themselves."[10] Therefore, insofar as we are willing to accept the more or less established usage that defines eros as the quintessence of all desire for fullness of being, for quenching of the thirst for happiness, for satiation by the good things of life, which include not only closeness and community with our fellow men but also participation in the life of God Himself — insofar as we do accept this usage, eros must be regarded as an impulse inherent in our natures, arising directly out of finite man's existence as a created being, out of his creatureliness. And when Karl Barth insists that man must "choose whether he wishes to love this way or that,"[11] either in the manner of eros or of agape, the question at once arises: Is man capable at all of so choosing? Choice implies being able to do otherwise. But can man do otherwise than, for example, want to be happy? Thomas Aquinas — whose importance here is less that of an individual writer than as the voice of humanity's traditional wisdom — answered this question many times with a decided "no":

man cannot do otherwise. "By nature the creature endowed with reason wishes to be happy and therefore cannot wish not to be happy."[12]

In this formulation we should not ignore the explicit reference to man's creatureliness. Of course Thomas's dictum does not constitute a defense for every random whim and every asserted "need for happiness." Not at all. But still something has been said that is fraught with many consequences for the theme of eros and agape — especially, for example, that the call for an utterly disinterested, unmotivated, sovereign agape love which wishes to receive nothing, which is purged of all selfish desire, simply rests upon a misunderstanding of man as he really is. The error, it must be noted, consists not so much in mistaking man's empirical imperfection as in failing to recognize that the *conditio humana* is that of a created being. Thomas and the tradition of thought represented by him do not merely accept as a fact the idea of man's craving happiness by nature as a symptom of persisting human weakness. Rather, he holds that this desire, directed toward quenching the deepest of thirsts, is not only entirely "in order," but is the indispensable beginning of all perfection in love.

On the other hand, the denigration of the human desire for happiness, which is implicit in contempt for eros, clouds and distorts any clear view of the phenomenon of love. In fact neither the one attitude nor the other can legitimately claim derivation from that Christian viewpoint which has shaped our thinking down to its barely conscious roots and down to our spontaneous forms of expression. This clarification, this recapture of an insight that the great tradition of European thought never lost, also clears the way for us to see once more the fundamental fact: that all love has joy as its natural fruit. What is more, all human happiness (which we instinctively desire, but not necessarily selfishly and therefore with rightfully clear

consciences) is fundamentally *the happiness of love,*
whether its name is eros or caritas or agape, and whether
it is directed toward a friend, a sweetheart, a son, a neighbor, or God Himself.

The happiness of love, lover's bliss, happiness in love,
or even *happiness with love* — these are, as everyone
knows, fairly ambiguous ideas. In ordinary language they
have undergone a rampant growth of meanings, and first
of all need a bit of pruning. For the present we shall not
go into the question of luck in love, that is, of the good
fortune of finding the right partner. That certainly exists,
and there is nothing whatsoever to be said against it —
although it obviously makes a difference whether what a
man is seeking and finding is the woman for the rest of
his life ("until death do us part") or what Harvey Cox[13]
calls a "Playboy accessory." But we are speaking of something else, of the essential relationship that connects happiness and joy with love, a relationship that, as will become apparent, is not so unequivocal as we might think
on first consideration.

Joy is by its nature something secondary and subsidiary.
It is of course foolish to ask anyone "why" he wants to
rejoice; and so it might be thought that joy is something
sought for its own sake, and consequently *not* secondary.
But if we look into the matter more closely it becomes
apparent that man, if all works out as it should, does not
want to plunge absolutely and unconditionally into the
psychological state of rejoicing but that he wants to have
a reason for rejoicing. "If all works out as it should"! For
sometimes things do not work out as they should — for
example when in the absence of a "reason" a "cause" is
brought to bear by a kind of manipulation, a pretext that
does not result in real joy but artificially produces a deceptive, unfounded feeling of joy. Such a cause may be
a drug or it may be the electric stimulation of certain
brain centers. Julian Huxley has argued that "after all,

electric happiness is still happiness";[14] but for the time being I remain convinced that St. Augustine correctly defines the true state of affairs — as well, incidentally, as expressing the viewpoint of the average man — when he says, "There is no one who would not prefer to endure pain with a sound mind than to rejoice in madness."[15] Man can (and wants to) rejoice only when there is a reason for joy. And this reason, therefore, is primary, the joy itself secondary.

But are there not countless reasons for joy? Yes. But they can all be reduced to a common denominator: our receiving or possessing something we love — even though this receiving or possession may only be hoped for as a future good or remembered as something already past. Consequently, one who loves nothing and no one cannot rejoice, no matter how desperately he wishes to (this is the situation in which the temptation to self-deception by constructing "artificial paradises" gains force).

Up to this point the intimate connection between love and joy seems to be a clear, uncomplicated matter. We desire something that we "like" and "love" — and then we receive it as a gift. Something that we tried to bring about by loving effort — we call this "love's labor" — finally succeeds (a scientific proof, the breeding of a new variety of rose, a poem). Then there is the story of the two prisoners of war in Siberia who ask themselves when people are truly happy and what makes them so, and who arrive at the conclusion: being together with those whom they love.[16] In all these examples the link between love and joy is direct and convincing. The much-cited "joy of being loved" is also a relatively clear though not entirely "pure" case — because some alien elements might well adulterate the joy of having someone else say, "How wonderful that you exist" (elements such as gratified vanity, confirmation of status — and so on).

But what about the joy of loving itself, that is, the joy that consists in loving? On the one hand, we have only to have the experience to immediately affirm, "Yes, this joy certainly does exist!" But then how can joy be something secondary, be the response to receiving or possessing something beloved? My answer to this question would be: Because we love to love! In fact we actually are receiving something beloved *by loving*. Our whole being is so set that it wants to be able to say with reason, "How good that this exists; how wonderful that you are here!" The "reason," of course, the only reason that seems cogent to our own minds must be that the existence of those praised things or persons actually *is* "good" and "wonderful." As has already been said, in this is manifested the "solid" aspect of the context of life as a whole: that the indivisibility of love and joy is not a delusion, wherein two separate emotions or physiological stimuli only seem to merge, but is in fact a response to reality — primarily, of course, to the real suitability to one another of human beings who feel "good" toward each other. They were indeed created for one another. Once again we are reminded, in a fresh way, that love has the nature of a gift: not only being loved, but also loving. And the element of gratitude, which is already present in the first stirrings of love, now becomes somewhat more comprehensible. It is gratitude that we are actually receiving what we by nature long for and love: to be able wholeheartedly to "approve" of something, to be able to say that something is good.

We must not allow this perception, which reflects the way Creation is fundamentally constituted, to be thrust off onto some innocuous, poetic sidetrack (although on the other hand Goethe's well-known lines, "Happy alone/Is the soul who loves"* is incomparably precise and realistic).

---

*The last lines of the poem, "Freudvoll und leidvoll."

Perhaps if we look at the reverse of the coin we will come to a better understanding of this difficult matter. The reverse is the inability to love, fundamental indifference, "the despairing possibility that nothing matters."[17] The true antithesis of love is not hate, but despairing indifference, the feeling that nothing is important.[18]

Despair is to be taken here more literally than it might seem. The radical attitude of "not giving a damn" in fact is in some way related to the state of mind of the damned. In Dostoevsky's novel *The Brothers Karamazov* Father Zossima says: "Fathers and teachers, I ponder 'What is hell?' I maintain that it is the suffering of being unable to love. Once in infinite existence, immeasurable in time and space, a spiritual creature was given, on his coming to earth, the power of saying, 'I am and I love.' "

Should anyone find this too mystical or too theological, perhaps he will be more impressed by what a German writer of these present times, returned home from exile, has to report concerning his direct experience. Though phrased more personally, it is basically no different from the Russian monk's wisdom. "During this time I experienced two kinds of happiness," he writes in summing up his feelings upon his return home. "The one was being able to help, to alleviate suffering. The other, and perhaps it was the greatest and most blessed happiness that has ever come my way, was: *Not to have to hate.*"[19]

But is there not such a thing as "*unhappy* love?" And if so, what light does that shed upon the seemingly plausible correlation of love and joy?

Let us say, by way of leaping ahead somewhat, that unhappy love not only exists as a fact, but that lovers alone can be unhappy. "Never are we less protected against suffering than when we love," says Sigmund Freud;[20] and an American psychologist actually calls love itself "an experience of greater vulnerability."[21] This has been known, and expressed, forever and a day; we may find it said in Thomas a Kempis's *Imitatio Christi*[22] and also, of course, in C. S. Lewis's book on love, which we have already quoted several times: "Love anything, and your heart will certainly be wrung and possibly be broken. If you want to make sure of keeping it intact, you must give your heart to no one, not even to an animal."[23] Obviously only a lover can have the experience of not receiving or of losing something loved; and that means being unhappy. Moreover, the failure to receive or the loss can be experienced as something in the present, or it can be remembered, or it can even be anticipated in despair. The inability to mourn rests upon inability to love.

Of course not receiving what we love can occur in a great variety of ways besides the one we are first inclined to think of: unrequited love in which the beloved turns away. The mystics likewise speak of this anguish: God is silent; He does not show Himself. They call it "aridity" and "the sterile season." But another possibility is that the beloved being falls upon evil ways and commits wrongs. Then, too, the lover is bound to be unhappy, since loving another means wishing that everything will work out entirely well for the beloved, that the beloved will be "all right," not just happy, but perfect and good.

Then where do we stand? Do both principles apply simultaneously: love and joy belong together, but love and sorrow likewise — just as Thomas Aquinas says with his cool objectivity: *ex amore procedit et gaudium et tristitia*,[24] "out of love comes joy as well as sadness"? Is it a simple matter of both this and that? No, it is not quite so simple.

First: There can of course be love without pain and sorrow, but love without joy is impossible. Second, and this is the main thing: Even the unhappy lover is happier than the non-lover, with whom the lover would never change places. In the fact of loving he has already partaken of something beloved. What is more, he still has a share in the beloved who has rejected him, been ungrateful to him, gone astray, or in some other way caused him grief. He has that share and keeps it, because the lover in some way remains linked with, remains one with, the beloved. Even unhappy or unrequited love has broken through the principle of isolation on which "the whole philosophy of hell rests"[25] and so has gained a solid basis for joy, a part no matter how small of "paradise."

In the light of this it becomes clearer why so many attempts to define love mention joy as an essential component of the concept. Here I am not thinking principally of that famous or notorious characterization, cast in the form of a geometrical theorem, to be found in the long list of definitions in Spinoza's *Ethics*: "Love is joy with the accompanying idea of an external cause."[26] This is a dubious, not to say disturbing, definition on a number of grounds. Suppose we were playing a guessing game and put this question: What is joy with the accompanying idea of an external cause? Who would ever guess that the answer was supposed to be love? And as a matter of fact Spinoza's definition has run into heavy criticism. Alexander Pfänder remarks that it indicates "very crude psychology"[27] and that "its complete wrongness" is easy to perceive.[28] Schopenhauer goes so far as to cite Spinoza's definition merely "for amusement, because of its extraordinary naiveté."[29] For my own part, I would point out that this "definition" does not even make it apparent that purely in terms of elementary grammar "to love" is a transitive verb, that is to say, a verb that must be linked with a direct object. To love always implies to love *someone* or *something*. And if this element is missing in a definition, it has failed to hit its target.[30]

Leibnitz gives a magnificent characterization of love — and, moreover, in a context in which we would scarcely expect to find it. In his *Codex iuris gentium diplomaticus* he writes, "To love means to rejoice in the happiness of another."[31] But of course we must ask, "But what if the other is not happy?" And later, in his *Nouveaux Essais*, Leibnitz offers a more precise formulation: To love means to be inclined to rejoice in the perfection, in the goodness or in the happiness of another."[32] That comes very close to the heart of the phenomenon, and does not differ so greatly from the exclamation: How good that you exist!

A century earlier St. Francis de Sales said almost the same thing, although his phraseology is just a shade more exact. Love, he declares in his *Traité de l'amour de Dieu*,[33] is *the* act in which the will unites and joins with the joy and the welfare of someone else.

If we consider our own experience with people, we will in fact realize that shared joy is a more reliable sign of real love than shared grief, or compassion; it is also far more rare. We need not agree with the Duc de La Rochefoucauld's cynical aphorism that there is something not altogether displeasing to us in our best friends' misfortunes. But it is evident that a good many foreign elements having nothing to do with love may be involved in compassion — which, therefore, is not so "pure" a case as shared joy.

Immanual Kant is so constituted that he basically mistrusts everything done out of "inclination," that is, out of joy. To him respect for duty is the only serious moral feeling.[34] ("Man is aware with the greatest clarity that he . . . must completely separate his desire for happiness from the concept of duty."[35]) For Kant "laboriousness" is the standard of all moral values. Yet even Kant is forced to recognize the relationship of love and joy: the fact of the matter is simply too compelling. His firm emphasis on doing as the true proof of love merits attention and respect, and we should not dismiss him too rapidly for his inflexible severity. After all, the New Testament contains some sentences that sound a similar note: "If you love me, you will keep my commandments" — John, 14:15.

And so there is much to be said for Kant's comment: "To love one's neighbor means to do all of one's duty toward him *gladly*."[36] But what is meant by this *gladly* — the emphasis is Kant's in the Critique of *Practical Reason?* Of course it means nothing less than: with joy.

VII

IF LOVE, THE desire for happiness, and joy are so closely intertwined, should it not be conceded that all love is a form, no matter how sublimated, of self-love? But how can that idea be reconciled with the other conviction, which likewise strikes us as self-evident, that genuine love never seeks its own?

In order to achieve some clarity on this question we shall have to recall once more something difficult to grasp, that even the acts of man's mind, which means even his volition and not just his sensual desires, take place *by nature* and thus are not something at our own command. Rather, such acts happen over our heads, as it were; they are not left to our freedom of choice but have already *been* imposed. We find this difficult to grasp because we usually understand the terms Nature and Mind as mutually exclusive concepts. According to this habit of thought, for example, willing is either a mental act, and consequently something not given by nature; or it is a natural event and consequently neither an act of volition nor a mental act at all. In contrast to this, the great teachers of Christendom unanimously insist that there is *one* being — that is in the strictest sense both Mind and Nature at once; and this being is the created mind.

We cannot repeat it too often: What happens "by nature" happens "by virtue of Creation"; that is, on the one hand it springs from the creature's inmost and most personal impulse; on the other hand the initial momentum for this impulse does not come from the heart of this same created being, but from the act of *creatio* which set in motion the entire dynamics of the universe. We might say it (the initial momentum) comes "from elsewhere" — if the Creator were not more within us than we ourselves. Anyone, therefore, who fully grasps and consistently applies the concept of creatureliness is forced to realize that at the core of the created mind and at the heart of its vital activity something happens that is entirely its own, and therefore a mental act, but simultaneously an event by virtue of creation, and consequently a natural process.

The functioning of *eros* is exactly of this kind — insofar as we mean by eros the desire for full existence, for existential exaltation, for happiness and bliss: a desire that cannot be diverted or invalidated and that naturally dominates and permeates all our emotions and all our conscious decisions, above all our loving concern for the world and for other human beings. Once more, then: "Man desires happiness naturally and by necessity."[1] To desire to be happy is not a matter of free choice."[2] Happiness can virtually be defined as the epitome of all those things which "the will is incapable of not willing."[3]

It is not in the least surprising that at this point, in regard to the interpretation and evaluation of eros, opinions differ. We should expect nothing else. Once more it is apparent that a conception of man must underlie any ideas about love. Anyone who maintains that man (and therefore himself also) is an absolutely free, non-necessitous,[4] autonomous being — at least in the life of his mind — must hold certain corollary views. He cannot regard

81

the will as incapable of not willing its own completion and fulfillment — these being only alternative terms for happiness. Anything else would seem to him a degradation of the autonomous subject. On the other hand, one who comprehends man to the depths of his soul as *creatura* simultaneously knows that in the act of being created we are — without being asked and without even the possibility of being asked — shot toward our destination like an arrow. Therefore a kind of gravitational impulse governs our desire for happiness. Nor can we have any power over this impulse because we ourselves *are* it.

Nevertheless this does not mean that man is consequently "by nature" an impotent nullity for whom God, as ultimately the only self-motivating force, must leap into the breach. The freedom of our own personal choices emerges from the very ground of what is willed by nature; and in this very process of willing by nature it is we ourselves, from the heart of our hearts, as it were, who desire happiness, desire our own happiness, of course.

In saying this we have formally returned to our theme. This desire for existential fulfillment, acting in us by virtue of Creation, is really "self-love." It is the basic form of love, which all others are founded on and which makes all others possible. At the same time it is the form of love most familiar to us from our inner knowledge of ourselves. Let us first consider this fact carefully. Then, perhaps, we may understand somewhat better why the love with which we love ourselves can be the standard for all other kinds of love. Granted, it sounds at first rather odd, and almost like a deliberate provocation, that self-love should serve as a paradigm from which we may read off what love in general is. But suppose we once more apply our "test" formula: It's good that you exist. To whom do we refer that expression, instantly and with sincerity, if not to ourselves? We do so even if at the moment we have been critically examining ourselves and do not find ourselves especially lovable. The spontaneous answer to this question seems to me so unequivocal that it hardly needs to be put into words. But of course it ill comports with the idea that love is equivalent to unselfishness.

Perhaps we are always engaged in somewhat repressing this truth, which strikes us as somehow unseemingly. At any rate, we may be surprised by the blunt statements of the ancients on this point. Consider, for example, these sentences from Aristotle's *Nichomachean Ethics*: "The relations which serve to define the various kinds of friendship seem to be derived from our relations to ourselves."[5] And: "The highest form of friendship can be likened to self-love."[6] Thomas Aquinas, too, mentions loving friendship and self-love in one breath: "A friend is loved as one for whom we desire something; and man also loves himself in exactly this same way."[7] We might at first take this analogy as meaning that self-love is a kind of image of friendship, that we love ourselves as we love a friend. But Thomas means just the opposite: friendship is the image and self-love is the original; we love our friends as we love ourselves. The derivative[8] element is the love for others: "it proceeds from the similarity to the love we bear ourselves."[9]

As has been said, such a statement leaves us considerably puzzled and inclined to object that strictly speaking a man is not his own friend. After all, we don't feel friendship for ourselves! Thomas Aquinas agrees: "We do not feel friendship for ourselves, but something greater than friendship . . . Everyone is at one with himself; and this *being* one is more than *becoming* one [*unitas est potior unione*]. Just as unity is closer to the source than union, so the love with which a person loves himself is the origin and the root of friendship. For the friendship that we have for others consists in this, that we behave toward them as we do toward ourselves."[10] Of course that statement is not intended, as it is in Voltaire,[11] as a cynical unmasking of purported unselfishness. However, we are being asked soberly to accept the fact that: "Everyone loves himself more than others."[12] That is simply so, nor is there anything wrong about it; it's not a matter of human weakness. It is so on the basis of our creatureliness, that is, by virtue of the immutable fact that in the act of being created we were launched irresistibly toward our own fulfillment, toward our felicity too, toward the full realization of what was intended for us — or as it is put in Christendom's sacred Book: "For God created all things that they might be" (Wis 1:14). Thomas cited this sentence and discoursed upon it many times, showing that in spite of the reference to the *Nichomachaean Ethics*[13] he is not speaking simply as an Aristotelian (which in fact he never was, strictly speaking[14]). Augustine makes precisely the same point: "If you do not know how to love yourself you cannot truthfully love your neighbor."[15] And in *The City of God*[16] he says that the lover receives the standard, the *regula* for love of neighbor, from himself, from his love for himself. Of course Augustine does not refer back to Aristotle, whose writings were scarcely known to him, but to the New Testament, which likewise establishes self-love as the measure for all love among human beings: Thou shalt love thy neighbor *as thyself*!

Incidentally, we will sometimes find the realistic attitude underlying this idea expressed from an altogether different angle in British and American writing on the subject of love. Self-love, it is argued, may very well sometimes assume the functions of rational judgment and protect purported or truly disinterested love from hurling itself to destruction for the sake of some idol. Truly loving devotion, the argument continues, always presupposes that the self and its dignity are not really threatened; only then can the lover freely and unreservedly, without a backward glance, surrender himself.[17] The complexities of the problem, which are implicit in the matter itself, can scarcely ever be reduced to handy solutions and formulas. Our line of argument should make that quite apparent.

It is all the more important, therefore, to understand what is meant by setting "self-love" as the standard for the love directed toward all other human beings and perhaps even toward God Himself. How then do we love ourselves?

It seems to me crucial that in loving affirmation of ourselves we always regard ourselves as *persons*, that is, as beings existing for their own sake. Even when we are finding fault with ourselves we think and judge in terms of our own impulses, fears and goals, our inner motivations. And this is precisely what we do not do when, in a state of pure desire, we cast our glance upon another person like an object, seeing that person as a mere provoker of stimuli, a means to an end. This point, incidentally, was also formulated by Aristotle in the *Nichomachean Ethics*.[18] Above all, Aristotle says, man really wishes the good for himself, whatever his concept of that good may be; he wishes it for himself and at the same time makes a reality of it for the sake of his own self. Moreover, we also wish the good as the persons we are now. In other words, we do not say: first I must change and become a different person, and then, when I "deserve" it more, I will wish good for myself. On the contrary, we say: I want it now, just as I am at the present moment — whether or not I happen to like myself right now. Loving, we remarked earlier, is not the same as liking. C. S. Lewis comments that for a long time he found it sheer hairsplitting that we are asked to hate sin but to love the sinner — until one day he realized that there was actually one person in the world toward whom he had followed that precept all his life, namely himself.[19]

Another idea in the *Nichomachean Ethics* may at first appear too obvious: that in loving ourselves we like to spend time with ourselves, both dwelling on memory and looking to the future. But to translate these obvious facts, in practical terms, into relationships with fellow men is just as difficult as — as love of neighbor (by which at this point we do not intend anything specifically Christian; what we mean is that attitude by which concern for another human being, including the partner in an erotic relationship, develops into "love").

It now appears that two separate ideas have crept into our discussion and become entangled: first, self-love, desire for happiness, striving for fulfillment as the root of all other love, the original source of love by nature. Second, self-love as the model and standard of love for others. But in both cases the question arises: How do we escape from love of ourselves — however much it may be the root or the model? How can we conceive this step to be taken? Or is it less a step than a leap, which sooner or later has to be taken, across the gulf that separates eros from agape?

After all, we do not have to accept Anders Nygren's extremist characterization of agape to realize that selfish love is not real love. And also to agree with Augustine when he states: "What is not loved for its own sake is not loved at all";[20] and: "When you love, love without recompense."[21] Everyone knows that from his own direct experience. Even Nietzsche, who spends a great deal of wit unmasking the "dreadful nonsense" that "love ought to be something 'unegoistical,'"[22] who calls love "this subtlest avarice"[23] and says of the lover that he is "more egoist than ever"[24] — even Nietzsche admits that when hearing the word "love" even "the slyest woman and the meanest man think of the relatively most unselfish moments of their entire lives."[25]

But precisely at this point the possibility of establishing a link appears, or at any rate a glimmering of what might be the nature of that step from self-love to disinterested or "selfless" love. Were not those most unselfish moments, of which both the slyest and the meanest persons think, also the happiest moments in their lives *because* of being the most unselfish? If eros, self-love, is basically the desire for happiness, then the question must be: what does happiness truly mean, and in what does it consist?

By way of a forewarning, we should say that no one can answer this question simply by giving a "positive" description of happiness. On this point Plato's view accords completely with that of Thomas Aquinas. In Plato's *Symposium*[26] the point is made that the soul of the lover evidently craves something else beside sexual pleasure, a something "which she cannot tell, and of which she has only a dark and doubtful presentiment." And Thomas declares, "By felicity everyone understands a state perfect to the highest degree; but in what this state consists is hidden."[27] Furthermore we know from our own experience that we certainly are not made happy by receiving what at first glance we seem really to have longed for. Ernst Bloch's phrase about the "melancholy of fulfillment" is pertinent here.[28] Kierkegaard, too, says many times that one who insists upon pleasure has set his foot on the road to despair. On the other hand, if it is true that joy and happiness are our response to partaking of something we love; and if loving, simple approval, is something beloved in itself — then it must likewise be true that our desire for happiness can be satisfied precisely by such affirmation directed toward another, that is by "unselfish" love. As Goethe puts it: "True happiness really consists only in sympathy."[29] At this point we must recall Leibnitz's definition that the essence of love consists in shared joy. This is how, he adds, "a difficult complication" is resolved, "namely how disinterested love, *amor non mercenarius*, can exist . . . For the happiness of those whose betterment gives us joy forms a part of our own happiness."[30]

Our initial question was how we might imagine the step from mere self-love to unselfish love that seeks nothing for itself. From all we have been discussing so far, we might draw the following conclusions: that no gulf separates the one kind of love from the other, at least not necessarily; that on the contrary it might be almost impossible to say where one's own desire for happiness ceases and unselfish joy in the happiness of others begins. Obviously there can be countless pretexts for self-deception, for covering up, and for subtle falsification but that only proves how fluid are the boundaries between eros and agape.

Even if agape (caritas) is explicitly identified as "supernatural," that is as a "virtue" which is nourished not by our own strength alone but by some divine power communicated to us through Grace, it still must not be thought of as strictly separated from nature-given self-love directed toward happiness and the fulfillment of existence. Such separation is only possible for one who holds, like Anders Nygren,[31] that creation and redemption have nothing to do with one another. Otherwise, on the contrary, we are rather prepared to find what is "by nature," that is, "by virtue of creation," strictly ethical matters, and the supernatural, so closely interwoven that the seam can scarcely be detected. Or at least it cannot so long as all three impulses, that which springs from nature, that which springs from ethical freedom, and that which springs from Grace, are in harmony with one another. If you row your boat in the same direction as the wind is driving it — how are you to distinguish between the motion that is due to your own efforts and what is due to the wind?

Earlier I referred to Leibnitz's phrase, *amor mercenarius*. This phrase, mercenary love, with its implication of the lover's always eying his reward, has repeatedly been applied to need-love, that is to eros, as a term of more or less summary contempt. But as might be expected, here too we are dealing with a rather complicated matter; and once more the dividing line between the meaningfully possible and the perversion *in concreto* is often enough scarcely discernible. Augustine added an explanatory sentence to his dictum, already cited, about true love's not asking compensation: "If you truly love, your reward must be he whom you love."[32] In other words, Augustine does maintain that there is a reward for love? But there can be more than one kind of "reward." Here Augustine uses the word *merces* (*ipse sit merces, quem amas*). This is a rather coarse word that sometimes carries the faintly contemptuous connotation of a day-laborer's wages, of payment, of paying off. But it is likely that he might have used the word in quotation marks, so to speak, possibly because he was addressing this sermon to the fishermen of Hippo. Elsewhere he says *praemium* and not *merces*: *Praemium dilectionis ipse dilectus*,[33] "the beloved himself is love's reward." *Praemium* can also be translated by "reward" and 'recompense," but unlike *merces* it also implies something not demandable, something that comes as a gift, even though it also comes as something intended and hoped for.

Of course we need not waste words making the point that what happens between the partners in "venal love," the kind that has its set price, has nothing to do with love. But what about the "reward" intended in real love, that reward which consists in the lovers' being together? Everyone who loves naturally wants this reward. But is that desire a selfish eying of compensation? Granted, the possibilities of illusion, self-deception and even of cynical misuse are, as we have said, legion. Even the reward implicit in lovers' being together can be misguidedly isolated so that eventually the embrace becomes, perhaps unintentionally, a means to a selfish end. When that happens the "lover" sets out on a course that ends with the alleged or supposed "beloved" no longer being regarded as a person at all, but as a thing, "as a machine to be used for his pleasure."[34]

For the present, however, we are speaking of the reward which comes with real love, or rather which is present along with it and it alone, as an immanent fruit. No one, it seems to me, has stated this matter so well as Bernard of Clairvaux. It is perhaps equally characteristic of him that his formulation comes from a treatise on the love for God,[35] and that it does not so much as mention the name of God. The sentence reads: "All true love is without calculation and nevertheless is instantly given its reward, in fact it can receive its reward only when it is without calculation . . . Whoever seeks as the reward of his love only the joy of love will receive the joy of love. But whoever seeks anything else in love except love will lose both love and the joy of love at the same time."

The paradoxical structure (and it is truly paradoxical) described here with magnificent simplicity recurs in all fundamental existential contexts. The indispensable goods of life can be acquired only by their being "given" to us; they are not accorded to use when we directly aim for them. One of the most important lessons of modern psychotherapy, for example, is that nothing so hampers the attainment of psychic health as the deliberate or exclusive intention to achieve or retain good health. As spiritual and ethical persons we must want to be "all right"; then such health will be given to us.

That love, insofar as it is real love, does not seek its own remains an inviolable truth. But the lover, assuming that he is disinterested and not calculating, does after all attain his own, the reward of love. And this reward, in its turn, and in view of human nature cannot be a matter of indifference to him.

I try to imagine the pleasure Augustine must have felt in arriving at this dialectical formulation (modeled on the biblical sentence about that special love which loses what it tries to keep): "If you love your soul, there is danger that it may perish. Therefore you are not permitted to love it, since you do not want it to perish. But in not wanting it to perish, you love it."[36]

VIII

HOWEVER DIFFERENT OUR definitions of love and however different in fact its manifold forms are, one element recurs in all descriptions of it and in all actualizations of it: the tendency toward union. Love is, as Dionysus Areopagita puts it, a *vis unitiva et concretiva* (*henotiké kai synkratiké*).[1] What happens in love among human beings is that two persons become one, so to speak, "So to speak" — for of course no one can actually become as closely united with any other person as he is with himself. Moreover, union in love presupposes that the elements of this new unit nevertheless remain distinct and independent: *unio est aliquorum distinctorum.*[2] Or as Jules Michelet elegantly puts it at the end of his famous though on the whole rather barren book: *Pour s'unir il faut rester deux,*[3] "It takes two to unite." The matter can also be expressed, with reversed accenting: Although the pair remain two, they become one. The paradox is unresolvable; it is inherent in the thing itself.

We have already cited C. S. Lewis's *The Screwtape Letters*, in which the argumentative devil pronounces it the sum of infernal philosophy that one thing is *not* the other and especially that one self is *not* another self —

whereas the philosophy of the "Enemy," that is God, amounts to nothing else but an incessant effort to evade this obvious truth. "He aims at a contradiction. Things are to be many, yet somehow also one. The good of one self is to be the good of another. This impossibility, He calls *love*."[4] That is something that does not exist in hell; in fact, as Dostoevsky's Russian monk says, its absence is precisely what makes up the essence of hell. Incidentally, the word "hell" need not necessarily imply something in the hereafter. If we may properly speak of heaven on earth,[5] then why not also of hell on earth?

But if this is so, if every form of love really and essentially seeks oneness and has union for its fruit,[6] then it must be said that such union, such merging of subjects who are nevertheless different from one another and remain so, finds its most complete realization in what is called erotic love. Consequently, love between the sexes becomes a paradigmatic form of love in general. Nevertheless, the concept of sexuality, which comes to mind as soon as love between man and woman is discussed, gives rise to a certain misunderstanding. For that reason we must speak somewhat more precisely.

Although obviously sexuality always plays a part in erotic love; although the human being, through all the levels of his individual life up to and including the style of his intellectual activity is either man or woman; although the biblical phrase about two who are made one flesh applies particularly to sexual union — it is nevertheless important, I think, to keep in mind something else that is likewise obvious and familiar to everyone. On the one hand the sexual act can take place without love and even without love in the narrower erotic sense. On the other hand, love between man and woman, understood as the closest imaginable union of persons, includes in addition to sexuality many quite other things — so much so that a sexuality set apart and therefore "absolutized" tends rather to block love, even erotic love, and to alienate people from one another as personal beings.

In the following discussion we are not, strictly speaking, dealing with what is usually described in "love stories" as *amour-passion.* Ortega y Gasset remarks in his essay on love that in all such stories "usually everything happens except the one thing that deserves to be called love in its proper sense."[7] However we want to speak here of love in its proper sense, which we define as the power that can produce a passionate merging not merely for the duration of an episode or an affair, but for a whole life ("till death do us part"), a union and communion embracing and permeating all the dimensions of existence. Integrated into that union and communion are all the forms and aspects of love among human beings — from sexual desire to supernatural agape. The decisive factor, as I see it, is precisely that all these elements enter into it; this, too, is what makes it paradigmatic: in such a communion of love there is no separation of eros and agape.

Incidentally, man does not wish to be loved "purely unselfishly." Not at all. Of course he wants to be affirmed and loved as a person, not just as the holder of certain qualities and abilities. In short, he wants to be loved for himself. But he is also concerned with being of value to the other and with being "used." Moreover, he definitely wants to be desirable, and certainly not just as an object of love unmotivated, value-neutral and solely-desirous-of-giving (the qualifications, we will recall, of that agape-love which Anders Nygren regards as the only kind appropriate for a Christian).

But erotic love can and actually has been discredited in other ways besides being pitted against theologically interpreted agape. We need only cite the grotesque terms in which Immanuel Kant, during the period he was writing the *Critique of Pure Reason,* disparaged the "sexual inclination": "Man certainly has no inclination to enjoy his fellow man's flesh, and where that is done, it is more an act of revenge in war than an inclination; but there remains one inclination in man which can be called an appetite and which aims at enjoyment of his fellow man. This is the sexual inclination." And he adds: "This cannot be love, but appetite."[8]

I have posited that the separation of erotic from ethical-supernatural love was a fateful thing fraught with many consequences. I have said that it was unrealistic because it ignores man's nature, that is, the condition imparted to him by virtue of his creation. And I have related the rift thus created between the two kinds of love to certain contemporary attitudes. This hypothesis might be extended. We might, for example, wonder whether the separation of eros from agape might not lead, almost of necessity, to that other aberration of love: namely, the isolation of sex from eros. It has been my observation that the integration of all aspects of the many-faceted phenomenon known as love, as it is experienced in the lifetime communion of man and woman, if everything goes as it should — that this integration is brought about and sustained by eros. In other words, to sum it up in an epigram, erotic love is the clamp that alone can hold together sex and agape. "He who despises eros succumbs to sex." That is another epigram (from Walter Schubart's sometimes problematical book, *Religion und Eros*[9]). But it seems to me that what is conveyed by these two pointed phrases calls for the most serious reflection. While we reflect, it is important to keep in mind the naturally *mediate* character of eros. Plato, too, laid stress on this aspect of eros in the *Symposium*[10]: Love "is intermediate between the divine and the mortal . . . ; he is the mediator who spans the channel which divides them, and therefore in him all is bound together." There is much to suggest that if this clamp which is called eros should fall away and be denied, the meaningful wholeness of human potentialities for love would instantly disintegrate.

But now the time has come to seek for a more precise meaning of eros and erotic love. Kant, Nygren, and Karl Barth place their emphases differently, but on the whole they are of one accord in saying that eros is really mere self-love, is "appetite."

I feel safe in going back to Plato, whom the abovementioned writers also claim to be following. Plato tends first of all to say that erotic love is something akin to poetic rapture, and in fact to artistic enthusiasm in general, a state of being carried out of the normality of everyday existence. In ordinary experience this quality is apparent in what we call infatuation: Ortega y Gasset wittily calls it an abnormal state of attention in a normal man.[11] But infatuation is not love; at most it is the beginning of love. Erotic love, too, is a kind of transport and rapture — the latter word literally meaning, as suggested above, being carried away by force out of the soul's normal state. The slang phrase, that a person is "gone on" someone, gets at the heart of the matter. This rapturous departure from the normality of everyday equilibrium happens, furthermore, upon encounters with physical beauty. Erotic love is kindled first and foremost by beauty — that is a commonplace.

But what does beauty mean? The old definition, which at first glance seems abstract and vague, is that beautiful means pleasing to look at. Yet the definition is apt insofar as it avoids pinning itself down. Beauty cannot be objectively defined or measured like any other "quantity." Is there any need to belabor the point that the "measurements" used in beauty contests are sheer commercialized idiocy? Nevertheless beauty is something distinctly sensual, or at any rate something that comes to the fore in the realm of the senses. But, as we have said, it escapes precise definition. When we try to characterize the beauty of a face that does not conform to any set pattern, we may speak of its charm; or we may call a certain way of speaking or moving "charming." But these words really mean no more than enchanting, enrapturing, transporting.

The difficulty, if not the impossibility, of a positive definition is perhaps connected with the fact that in experiencing sensual beauty we are being referred to something that is not simply present and discernible. What takes place within us at the sight of beauty is not really that we experience satisfaction of any sort, but rather something like the awakening of expectation. We do not see or partake of a fulfillment, but of a promise. Goethe summed it up in a marvellously succint phrase that, incidentally, reiterates Plato's view: "Beauty is not so much performance as promise."[12] That erotic love responds to just this promise-aspect of beauty — that has been recognized and expressed again and again. Paul Claudel has said: "Woman is the promise that cannot be kept; but it is precisely in this that my mercy consists."[13] And as might be expected, C. S. Lewis is quite familiar with the concept: "Eros is driven to promise what Eros himself cannot perform."[14]

What happens in erotic love is thus not "gratification" but an opening of the sphere of existence to an infinite quenching which cannot be had at all "here." Naturally this interpretation of eros is not to be taken as a simple description of the average situation, as though that is what actually happens at every encounter between Jack and Jill. But it is certainly not mere romanticizing. Rather, it indicates that we are vouchsafed something in all erotic emotion and rapture which we would otherwise never know — that we are drawn into something that goes infinitely far beyond what seems at first hand to be meant.

Naturally sexuality is always present in the erotic love of man and woman, and sexual union is also kept in view. Nevertheless, the specifically *erotic* quality of the relationship is of an entirely different kind. Perhaps we may even cast doubt on what Sigmund Freud[15] seems to be asserting:

that the sexual relationship is "primarily intended," and is only set aside or merely glossed over temporarily. In this connection Rollo May[16] refers to the examples of Antony and Cleopatra in Shakespeare's tragedy. Undoubtedly, May says, there were plenty of courtesans in the Roman army to satisfy the general's "sexual needs." But in the encounter with Cleopatra something wholly new suddenly happened; only then "Eros entered the picture, and Antony became transported into a whole new world." And in Goethe's novel *Werther* we are shown two persons who are clearly lovers and altogether man and wife; and yet Werther can say, "All desire is stilled in their presence."

Of course sensuality is involved, and so is sexuality; but these urges are neither isolated nor primary, at least not as long as the mediative daimon Eros reigns. All this has nothing whatsoever to do with "puritanism," "bourgeois morality," or any kind of ascetical disparagement of sexuality. Once more we may quote Goethe, who is hardly open to the charge of prudishness. Yet he makes this very distinction several times, even in his autobiography when he reports on his own earliest erotic experiences. Thus he writes in *Dichtung and Wahrheit*[17] (*Poetry and Truth*), "The first erotic leanings of unspoiled youth take an absolutely spiritual turn. Nature seems to desire one sex to perceive goodness and beauty sensuously embodied in the other sex. And so the sight of this girl, because of my affection for her, opened up to me a new world of beauty and excellence."

That is, as we see, not so very distant from what Plato says about Eros. But neither Goethe nor Plato deceives himself into thinking that he has thereby said everything there is to say about love, and certainly not everything about what constitutes the lifelong communion of man and wife. Plato especially — whom we lateborn and enlightened readers all too soon suspect of speaking too academically, that is "platonically," about love — Plato is actually quite free of illusions and hardly apt to slip into unrealistic attitudes. We need only read carefully what he puts into the mouth of Socrates concerning the brutality of the many or concerning the cultivated sensuality of a rationalized, technical approach to living — both attitudes fundamentally aiming at nothing but pleasure.[18] It is also true, however, that in the same dialogue, *Phaedrus*, we find the statement that eros which renounces sexual pleasure is the most blessed form of love.[19] Here is where doubts arise as to whether this is not a romantic, sentimental exaggeration. Still and all, Paul Claudel says, "Human love is beautiful only when it is not accompanied by gratification."[20] That is a profoundly problematic sentence, one that at any rate raises a number of fresh questions. But it can do no harm, I think, to consider from time to time that the man who could seriously hold this idea was a person of a certain stature.

To return to Plato for the moment, he knows perfectly well that the heroic form of love is a rarity that cannot be required of the average human being. Nevertheless he remains convinced that only the mediative power of erotic rapture can humanize naked desire, and that only such self-forgetfulness can preserve men from "the dark pathways." On the other hand: "He who is not a lover can offer a mere acquaintance flavored with worldly wisdom, dispensing a niggardly measure of worldly goods; in the soul to which he is attached he will engender an ignoble quality . . ."[21] But the same mediative daimon that alone can prevent the isolation of *sexus* from love is also able to keep allegedly pure ethical or spiritual "love" (which likewise is in constant danger of degenerating into inhumanity) from repressing the capacity for sensual upheavals and thus becoming a gloomy, an inflexible "charity without love."[22]

It is therefore not altogether incomprehensible that eros, viewed in such terms, should embody in its overall purest form the essence of love — *as long as it reigns.* But we must add this qualification. Granted, the word "forever" is quintessentially native to the vocabulary of eros. And it is by no means just "sounding brass." In the festive being-beside-oneself of erotic rapture time really stands still; there emerges something of that "suspended present" that in fact is an element in the concept of eternity. Yet even if we grant this, erotic love seems to unfold to the full blossoming of its beauty only for a short span of time, especially at the beginning, during the "first" encounter of lovers. Eros, it has been said, is "a preface by nature."[23] But if all goes well this preface will not be forgotten. It has set a standard, has established a stock that can never be used up. On the other hand, undoubtedly it is only realistic to call erotic love the notoriously "most mortal form" of love.[24]

But, once more: as long as eros reigns it embodies in purest form the complete essence of love. Then above all the "wonderful that you exist" springs most intensely from the heart, most blessed and blessing, and least contaminated by other elements.

In contrast to that statement we find, in Werner Bergengruen's posthumous autobiography, the elegiac sentence: "Love for children is perhaps the most intense love; for it knows that it has nothing to hope for."[25] But as a kind of response we might consider the words of Lacordaire: "It is an honor for you to find again in your children the same ingratitude you showed toward your own fathers, and thus attain to the perfection of loving, like God, without self-interest," with a *sentiment désinteressé.*[26] But the father's as well as the mother's love is naturally always mingled with other elements, such as concern and anxiety. Pure, unadulterated affirmation is, it seems, attained only in erotic love. Nowhere else, moreover, is the gift-nature of being loved as well as of loving and being permitted to love so intensely experienced. For the first and perhaps for the only time you spontaneously and effortlessly love

99

another person truly "as yourself."[27] And that is why such lovers cannot conceal their joy; they actually radiate it — very differently from mere sex partners who, as everyone has observed, tend to walk about looking rather frustrated and sullen. For a moment in erotic love the world of man is whole, hale, holy, and life has turned out good and happy. For that reason everyone is well-disposed toward lovers; "all mankind loves a lover."[28] Erotic love is also the theme of Georg Simmel's melancholy epigram that music and love are the only undertakings of mankind that are not hopeless from the start.[29]

If we consider all this, it will scarcely seem surprising that eros has repeatedly been deified. Of course the biblical sentence "God is love" (1 Jn 4:8) has nothing to do with such deification — quite aside from the fact that the New Testament text does not use the terms *eros* or *amor*, but *agape* and *caritas*. Nevertheless, the Christian tradition of European thought shows a constantly recurring stress on the "erotic" elements even in the love of God. I think it significant that the idea first expressed by Dionysius Areopagita, that the noun *eros* is "more divine" (*theioteron*) than the noun *agape*,[30] should be taken over centuries later by Thomas Aquinas in his famous textbook for beginners. To be sure, Thomas immediately offers an interpretation: because *amor* primarily means being carried away, he says, it is somewhat more divine than *dilectio*, which contains more of an element of rational selectiveness: *divinius est amor quam dilectio*.[31] And St. Francis de Sales also appeals to Dionysius Areopagita[32] when he defends the title of his treatise on the love of God; quite rightly, he says, the love of God is given the more excellent name of *amor*.[33]

We are dealing with something quite different when we consider the apotheosis of eros such as is to be found in, for example, Walter Schubart's already cited book *Re-*

ligion und Eros, which Karl Barth has called a "frightening book."[34] Schubart argues not only that "eroticism is a religious category,"[35] which in a sense might still be considered acceptable, but also that: "Religion and eroticism have the same goal,"[36] and: "Love between the sexes when impelled by the urge to redemption, and the love of God, are the same in their essence."[37] Here, clearly, we have a romantic obliteration of boundaries between two entirely different realms, and the result does justice to neither. On this point we must agree fully with Karl Barth's criticism, just as we agree with his sharply ironical condemnation of Schleiermacher's embarrassing "Intimate Letters concerning Friedrich Schlegel's *Lucinde*" and of Schlegel's own nonsense about the "sacredness of sensuality" and the "priests and liturgists" of the religion of Eros.[38] But it remains completely incomprehensible to me how a man like Karl Barth could have hit on the idea that the Catholic doctrine of the sacramental nature of marriage is in any way related to such deification of Eros.[39]

But let us consider something of greater importance and greater contemporary relevance than discursive theory. There seems nowadays some strong imperative to conduct ourselves as though eros really were a kind of absolute authority. There are those who feel that they are in the right, are carrying out a kind of religious duty "in the service of eros" — even though they may be deceiving a spouse, betraying a friend, abusing hospitality, destroying the happiness of others, or abandoning their own children. Then everything appears as a "sacrifice" painfully offered upon the altar of love.[40] C. S. Lewis with his magnificent metaphysical common sense has framed two memorable warnings in this connection. The first is: "When natural things look most divine, the demoniac is just round the corner."[41] And the second: "Natural loves that are allowed to become gods do not remain loves."[42]

In conclusion, nevertheless, we must say one word more in favor of erotic love. When people graced with mystical insight search for the figure of speech to communicate their directly incommunicable experiences in their dealings with the personal ground of their own existence, that is with God, they evidently can find nothing more appropriate than comparison with the ecstatic raptures of eros. Thus we find the language of love in both the Canticle of Canticles and in the writings of such mystics as Hugh of St. Victor. In his small book, *On the Love of the Bridegroom for the Bride*,[43] Hugh writes, "I will speak, He said, with my bride . . . And when I speak to the bride, ye shall know that I cannot speak of anything but love."

IX

THERE IS AN implication to calling Eros a mediative power that unites the lowest with the highest in man; that links the natural, sensual, ethical and spiritual elements; that prevents one element from being isolated from the rest; and that preserves the quality of true humanness in all the forms of love from sexuality to *agape*. The implication is that none of these elements can be excluded as inappropriate to man, that all of them "belong." The great tradition of Christendom even holds that those aspects of man that derive from his nature as a created being are the foundation for everything "higher" and for all other divine gifts that may be conferred upon him. "It is not the spiritual which comes first, but the sensuous-earthly and then the spiritual" — if one were unfamiliar with this quotation, one would scarcely guess that it comes from the New Testament (I Cor 15:46[1]). Furthermore, Thomas Aquinas, the last great teacher of a still undivided western Christendom says, "Were natural love (*amor*), or eros, not something good in itself, then *caritas* (*agape*) could not perfect it.[2] Rather, agape would have to discard and exclude eros (which Anders Nygren asserts that it does). That same tradition we call "western" in the specific sense of being not unworldly but rather characterized by a "worldliness" founded on a religious and theological basis[3] — that tradition speaks with complete matter-of-factness of sexuality as a good.[4] It says, with Aristotle, that there is something divine in the human seed.[5] And unresponsiveness to sensual joy, *insensibilitas*, is treated not only as a defect but also as a *vitium*, a moral deficiency.[6] On the other hand, the underlying conception implies that all of man's powers, and especially sexuality, can remain "right" and "in order" only in their natural place, which is to say within the wholeness of physical-spiritual-mental existence. Once again we call to mind the mediative and integrating functions of eros.

Everything that is intermediate naturally runs the risk of ambiguity; it can be misinterpreted in two directions. In the case of eros this emerges in a characteristic semantic instability of the words associated with it. *Desiderium*, for example, means both "longing" and "wanting"; significantly, "I want" can mean both "I lack" and "I wish for." The word *desire* which is derived from *desiderium*, means both "longing" and "lust." *Appetitus* may at one time mean a "striving toward," at another time "appetite." And from here it is only a step to the deprecatory judgment that eros is only a "coarser or subtler appetite."[7] With which we return to the subject of "disparagement of eros." This time it is disparagement from "above," from the viewpoint of a spiritual or supernatural conception of man. Eros is regarded as basically a more or less obvious disguise for purely selfish desire. A similar charge may also be made from "below," from the viewpoint of blunt instinctuality. Then, too, eros appears to be merely a mask, a wholly superfluous furbelow, sheer romantic affectation needlessly covering up what is really meant: a simple gratification of the instinctual drive.

Now that we have discussed the danger of separating agape from the wholeness of existence, we should have something to say about that other perversion which, as everyone knows, is especially prevalent today: making isolated sexuality into an "absolute."

A word of warning, though. Let us not exaggerate the gravity of "sexualization" as it supposedly affects the public nowadays. Too much of it comes down to commercial motives and the techniques of advertising. And although there has been talk of a "wave" — if there is one, we should conceive of it not so much like the natural waves of the ocean as like the mechanically produced movement of the water in a swimming pool. On the other hand, of course, the isolation of sexuality, as a form of potential human degeneracy, has always been with us. And it should be pretty apparent that it has existed both as a practice and as an outlook.

We come upon just such a situation in the Platonic dialogue that we have already cited several times. Young Phaedrus, who crosses Socrates' path, has an air of being dazzled and perhaps somewhat dazed. He has just come from a gathering of avant-garde intellectuals. Plato sees this group as marked by a speciously reasoned negation of traditional values, by a sophisticated life-style, by a deliberate surrender to instinctual drives. And Phaedrus, fascinated by the modernity and the eloquence of "the ablest writer of our day"[8] who had done the talking, tells Socrates about the pattern of action they propose. In briefest summary this pattern might be reduced to the following points: Lust without love. The aim should be a maximum of pleasure with a minimum of personal involvement. The erotic emotion, the *passio* of love, is considered a romantic disease that unnecessarily complicates everything. Refusal to let oneself be deeply affected is declared the sole "rational" kind of behavior; what is more, it is also extolled as really "decent," as *areté*.

As we can see, perhaps with some astonishment, these attitudes are uncannily topical today. Or, more precisely, they are attitudes human beings have evidently been able to form and adopt throughout the ages.

Socrates listens to it all for a while, at first pretending to the credulous Phaedrus that he too is enthralled by these ideas. Then, from one moment to the next, he abruptly drops the mask and puts an end to the game: Don't you see, my dear Phaedrus, how shameful all this really is?[9] Suppose a truly noble man had been listening to us now, one who loved another person as generous and humane as himself. Would not such a man surely think that we had been brought up among galley slaves and had never known love among free men?[10]

I trust we need not point out that this contrast between free men and galley slaves does not, despite appearances, have anything to do with the social reality of the Greek "slaveholders' society." What is meant here by slavery is a concept that no social changes, no emancipation, can wipe off the face of the earth. What is meant is something that, as the example of the Athenian upper crust shows, can quite naturally occur in all social classes: the ethically vulgar, plebian quality of such an attitude, and the barbarous crudity and brutality concealed behind all its civilized subtleties.

And now Socrates summons up before the astonished eyes of this ignorant young know-it-all, Phaedrus, the picture of the mediative daimon Eros. Much of what he says scarcely speaks directly to us nowadays; we can approach it only by a detour employing the interpretative tools of intellectual history. The crucial lesson is that in Eros sensuality fuses with spirituality and morality and, moreover, with what must be reckoned the gifts of God, into a unity. Here too, it must be granted, Plato's mythic imagery ("the soul acquiring wings") sounds somewhat sentimental and strange to us. But in reality something entirely realistic is meant. It comes pretty close to what Goethe was saying in his reference, cited above, about "the first erotic leanings of unspoiled youth": that Nature seems to be desiring it.[11]

I wonder how Socrates would have treated this Goethean statement, how he would have taken it into his hand and turned it round and round. Well, friends, what shall we say: Does uncorruptedness really exist? And what might be the difference between an uncorrupted and a — let us put it cautiously — a not uncorrupted youth?

For my part, I would answer this truly socratic question by drawing attention first of all to the fact of the word's *passive* form. Youth does not simply spoil the way butter turns rancid or milk sour. But — unfortunately — youth can be spoiled by someone else; that can very well happen. For example, it can be spoiled by seduction and commercial manipulation which contrary to the natural course of things acquaint it sooner with isolated sexual lust than with falling in love and love — so that sex enters youth's consciousness and life before eros does, and in such a way that experiencing real love is hampered if not blocked permanently.

Precisely this is what is so bad and so inhuman about sexual activity separated from eros: it frustrates the very experience that constitutes the meaning of the erotic encounter within the whole of existence. That experience is the escape from one's own limitations and egotism by union with another person. The mere sex partner does not come into focus as a personal being, that is, as a living self with an individually cast human countenance. An American has put the matter very wittily, remarking that where the "playboy" is concerned, the fig leaf has merely been moved to another place; it now covers the human face.[12] Actually, the man who is merely lustful does not, despite the usual phrase, want "a woman" at all. It is eros that wants a beloved woman and wants being together with her. Sex, on the contrary, seeks a neuter, something material and objective, not a "you" but an "it," the thing in itself (as the partners in Orwell's *1984* explicitly tell one another); the desire is "to do the thing" (as the phrase is in a novel by Heinrich Böll[13]). The encounter that is sheer sex and nothing else has rightly been called deceptive in character. For the moment an illusion of union arises; but without love this apparent union of two strangers leaves them more remote from one another than they were before.[14] Thus it should cause little surprise that "in a society which makes sexuality the prerequisite for love and not love the condition for the gift of physical union," sex paradoxically "rather separates that unites man and woman, leaving them alone and lonely precisely where they thought they would surely find each other."[15] As such sex-consumption increases, this effect is intensified and the sexual encounter becomes increasingly disappointing. The result, says Paul Ricoeur,[16] is not what Sigmund Freud's generation expected from the abolition of sexual "taboos" but rather the "forfeit of value by making intercourse free." Ricoeur points out, "Everything that makes the sexual encounter easy simultaneously speeds its collapse into insignificance." At bottom that is hardly surprising. It might be called an iron law. What can be had on demand and almost gratis, and almost at once as well (Americans use the robust expression "short order sex"[17]), necessarily loses both its value and its attractiveness. The head of the health center at an American state university, a psychiatrist by profession, reported that some of the more promiscuous girl students replied in answer to an inquiry, "It's just too much trouble to say 'No.' "[18] At first hearing that may sound like sheerest freedom but clearly it also means: I don't really care; it doesn't matter. The wholly inevitable result is already implicit: "sexuality not only without joy but without pleasure";[19] "so much sex and so little meaning or even fun in it."[20]

As I indicated, a universal law is operating here. Goethe in later life once put the matter thus, in a quite different context, "Every century . . . tries to make the sacred common, the difficult easy, and the serious amusing — to which there really could be no objection if it were not that in the process seriousness and amusement are destroyed together."[21] That's just it: the fun goes out of it too. And so it is grimly apt that the article by the university psychiatrist should be entitled: "The Roots of Student Despair."

We are certainly not dealing here merely with the consequences of a wanton abuse of freedom, at least not with that alone. The matter is not so simple. Along with the discussion of the devaluation of easy sex Rollo May also speaks of its nearly compulsive nature.[22] In the grayed world of a work-oriented society geared to output, sex seems to be the only remaining green thing.[23] David Riesman's well-known phrase has been echoed many times: sex is the last frontier, that is, the last still accessible realm of adventure, excitement and unregimented life. But once we fix our gaze upon this "sociological" aspect of the matter we have to ask whether a kind of vicious circle has not formed here, and one almost impossible to break out of. On the one hand "the one green thing"[24] in the midst of a world of labor that is more and more completely dominating man is love alone, eros, the rapturous affirmation of the beloved that makes for forgetfulness of self (or even the affirmation of any thing loved disinterestedly). And this true overstepping of the bounds of all functionalism aimed solely at utility and gratifying needs is also implicit, more or less obscurely, in sexual craving. On the other hand, this very thing that is truly longed for cannot be attained by detached, easy sex.

Max Horkheimer's remark in an interview, "We must pay for the pill with the death of erotic love,"[25] raised a good many hackles, but it contains an almost undeniable truth. However, it seems to me that the decisive factor is not, as Horkheimer implies, the dstruction of longing.

What is more decisive is that something in principle not freely available is to be made available at will, and "without risk." But of course this easily available thing cannot be what was really sought.[26] What is really sought, human closeness, overcoming of loneliness, union with another personal being — all that can be had only in real love. But at this point we see a further segment of the vicious circle. For love, above all eros, is by nature something that cannot be fitted smoothly and easily, without problems, into the functional context of utilitarian plans. "Eros is the one element in man that most intensely resists assimilation by the technological system."[27] On the other hand detached sex as a "consumer good," as a "ware," can be smoothly installed and planned into the great utilitarian organization — as has been persuasively described in a number of important literary visions of the future, such as Aldous Huxley's *Brave New World*.

But now another "on the other hand" must be considered, one that seems to close the vicious circle. Human personality forbids being "used" for the ends of others. Yet in consumer sex that deliberately fends off love the partner is regarded purely as a means and instrument. Hence the human face is not seen at all (this ignoring of the other may be quite mutual). Complete absence of human warmth is almost requisite. Consequently, in such detached sexuality there is hidden, despite all the outward show, a measure of frigidity[28] in the clinical sense of the word. There is also, insofar as the relationship of person to person is concerned, an element of violence, and a tinge of exactly that same "totalitarian coldness"[29] that pervades the atmosphere of dictatorships and of purely technocratic societies — in which there is no room for the "green thing" called love, so that again the human being is driven to the one seemingly open but in fact deceptive escape route of isolated sex consumption.

It is highly significant that in serious modern writing on the subject, for all the variety in philosophical or scientific approaches, the idea of the *demonic* comes up more or less explicitly. This idea has, of course, nothing to do with the Platonic conception of the "mediative daimon Eros"; on the contrary, it refers to an evil power that aims at dehumanization and destruction. Karl Barth has expressed it in a phrase that for him is unusually forceful: "Coitus without coexistence is a demonic affair."[30] Harvey Cox, equally unexpectedly, actually brings up the obsolescent concept of exorcising demons and driving out devils, although the word "exorcism" has already vanished from several theological dictionaries.[31] Because the dehumanization of life nowhere appears in more devastating form than in the modern sex industry, he says, nowhere else is "a clear word of exorcism more needed."[32] Physicians and psychologists speak of the underlying tendency to self-destruction involved in detached sexuality.[33] Only eros can preserve men from that, they say.[34] And C. S. Lewis puts a verse of John Donne as the terrifying motto of his book on love: "That out affections kill us not nor dye."[35]

Now it is part of the nature of the demonic power (in the strict sense of the word) that it never shows itself in its true form. Rather, it masquerades as sheer amusement and, above all, as an almost obligatory modernity — which, of course, magnifies its destructive effect. If only eros can give what is sought in sex, then this is precisely what "the shamans of sales" and "the sorcerers of the mass media and the advertising guild"[36] will try to deceive men about. The lie consists in this: that with an enormous expenditure of money (the whole thing is big business, after all), but also with the investment of tremendous psychological knowledge, with a maximum of skill in dealing with words and pictures, and with impressive subliminal use of music, color, form (and so on), the consumer is made to believe that sex is the same thing as eros and that all the gifts of eros, all the joyful raptures of "togetherness" can be had in sex consumption. It isn't offered for free, certainly not, but still it is basically available to everyone. The production of such deceptions has from ancient times been the business of the sophist, whom Plato in one of his late dialogues[37] described as a maker of fictive reality. The sophistic "art of persuasion" by flattery and propaganda creates the image of mass idols, or the illusion that smoking a particular cigarette will bring one "the pure joy of life" and "the fragrance of the great wide world." In the erotic realm the range of such sophistry extends from the suggestive slogans of advertising[38] to the department of *haute littérature*, as for example in the novels of D. H. Lawrence, who has already become rather old-fashioned. Of a couple celebrating the sexual act in the woods, Lawrence solemnly says: "They let themselves be carried away by the wave of life." On which C. S. Lewis dryly remarks: Since in these novels the characters never speak of possible fertility, neither in the terms of hope nor of fear, it must be assumed that they will allow themselves to be carried away by the wave of life only just so far as seems useful to them, and no farther.[39]

Such realistic reminders of what's what can serve as a form of "exorcism," as can the corrective irony of sober language. Socrates, as everybody knows, constantly made use of such techniques. But he also knew that such opposition was not sufficient. And so, thinking of the danger to young men of the type of Phaedrus, he asked the distrubing question, "When they huddle together in groups — in the theater, in court, in the camps — and express their displeasure or approval with tremendous noise, with clapping and shouting, and everything resounds with disapproval and applause — how do you think the young person will feel then? What an extraordinary education he will have had to receive in order to put up resistance and not be carried along with the current wherever it happens to be going. Ought we not to say: If he really liberates himself and thrives in healthy growth — that is owing to divine providence and is pure gift?"[40]

That is, as we can see, not so very different from a call to prayer. So, too, I have not the remotest notion of how Harvey Cox imagines that an "exorcism" is to be carried out in concrete form. But in using this word, he is introducing a clearly religious category and is indubitably right in doing so. He too is suggesting that the realm of sex and eros needs both purification and perfection by a superhuman power.

X

So FAR WE have spoken not at all about several aspects of the phenomenon known as "love." One such, for example, is friendship, or more exactly, the love of friends. That is in fact a special form of love, though one that nowadays, oddly enough comes in for little praise, whereas Aristotle devoted to it one entire book of the ten books that make up his *Nicomachean Ethics*. Friendship takes time, he says there;[1] it is normally not kindled just by the sight of the other, but by the surprise at discovering that here is someone else who "sees things exactly" the way one sees them oneself, someone of whom one can say happily, "It's good that you exist!" Friends do not gaze at each other, and totally unlike erotic lovers they are not apt to talk about their friendship. Their gaze is fixed upon the things in which they take a common interest. That is why, it has been said, people who simply wish for "a friend" will with fair certainty not find any. To find a friend you first have to be interested in something.[2] Although, therefore, real intimacy does not exist in friendship a friend is perhaps the only human being in whose presence we speak with complete sincerity and "think aloud"[3] without embarrassment.

So far we also have not spoken directly of the distinctive

114

qualities of maternal love. It has always been said that mothers, as those who love most intensely, seek less to be loved than to love.[4] A mother's love for her children is "unconditional" in a unique fashion; that is, it is not linked with any preconditions. Because of that it corresponds to the deepest longings of children, and indeed of every human being.[5] Maternal love doesn't have to be "earned"; and there is nothing anyone can do to lose it. A father, on the contrary, tends to set conditions; his love has to be earned. But that likewise repeats a fundamental element peculiar to all love: the desire that the beloved not only "feel good" but that things may in truth go well for him. A mature person's love must, as has rightly been remarked,[6] contain both elements, the maternal and the paternal, something unconditional and something demanding.

And so there may well be an untold number of possible ways for human beings to feel good toward one another, to like each other, to feel closeness and affection for one another. But varied as these forms and unsystematic as these degrees of fondness, attachment, liking and solidarity obviously may be, they all have one thing in common with friendship, parental love, fraternity, and specifically erotic love: that the lover, turning to the beloved, says, "It's good that you are here; it's wonderful that you exist!" (Unexpectedly we see once more that mere sex partnership cannot be included in this category — because in such partnerships there is no trace of a "you"; there is an ego, and maybe there are two egos, but there is no "you" involved!)

The fundamental affirmation that recurs in identical form in all real love is, as we said at the very beginning of our reflections, by its nature and quite apart from the lovers' awareness of it, the re-enactment of something else that precedes it. It is an imitation of the divine creative act by virtue of which the human being we have just encountered, who suits us and who seems "made for us," exists; by virtue of which, in fact, all reality exists at all and is simultaneously "good," that is, lovable.

But this aspect of the phenomenon of love, which admittedly points beyond empirically knowable reality, must be considered more closely once more — in order for us to be able to name and grasp another special form of love that we have hitherto said nothing about, at any rate not explicitly, but that most certainly cannot be overlooked. Not that we have any intention of going into theology! A theological book on love, that is one interpreting the documents of the sacred tradition and revelation, would undoubtedly have to deal with entirely different matters from those we are now about to discuss. No, we shall keep our eyes fixed upon the phenomenon of love as we encounter it in our experience. The question is, however, whether we may not, by dint of including in our considerations something that belongs to the realm of belief, be able to clarify and interpret a fact of experience that would otherwise remain obscure and uncomprehended.

There is, for example, to pitch our discussion in concrete terms at once, the quite empirical contemporary phenomenon of Mother Teresa,[7] the Yugoslav nun in Calcutta who has recently been receiving a considerable amount of publicity. She taught English literature in her order's high school for girls. One day she could no longer endure seeing, on her way to school, deathly ill and dying people lying in the street without receiving any humane aid. She therefore persuaded the city government to let her have an empty, neglected pilgrims' rest house and in it established her subsequently famous Hospital for the Dying. I have seen this shelter, which at the beginning was a most dismal place. Of course people die inside it likewise — but now they need no longer perish amidst the bustle of the streets. They feel something of the presence of a sympathetic person.

On the one hand what can we call this work of mercy but a form of loving concern, nourished by the fundamental impulse of "It's good that you exist" and affecting the loving person not just on a supernatural or spiritual level detached from all natural emotions. Rather, it affects him through all the levels of his being. *On the other hand* something new and fundamentally different is taking place here, or at any rate something that cannot so easily be reduced to a common denominator with friendship, liking, fondness, being smitten — and so on.

I should like to try, step by step, to make this new element seem plausible, to show how it is something lying within man's potential, or more precisely, something that has been put within the scope of human feeling. The first step, without our knowing it, has already been taken. It consists in our re-enacting, whenever we love, the primal affirmation that took place in the Creation. But it would also be possible that — taking the second step — we "realize" deliberately this iterative aspect of our loving. When we find something we see good, glorious, wonderful (a tree; the structure of a diatom seen under the microscope; above all, of course, a human face, a friend, one's partner for the whole of life, but also one's own existence in the world) — when we see something good, I say, when we love something lovable, we might become aware of our actually taking up and continuing that universal approval of the Creation by which all that has been created is "loved by God" and is therefore good. It would be a further step, beyond the mere recognition of this truth, to wish to observe it expressly, as if we were joining in with the Creator's affirmative and allying ourselves with it in a sort of identification — joining with the primordial act of affirmation and also with the "Actor." We might, in other words, for our part also love the "First Lover." Obviously that would change our own love for things and people, especially for those whom one loves more than all others; our own love, that is, would receive a wholly new and literally absolute confirmation. And the beloved, though still altogether incomparable, still someone personally and specially intended for us, would at the same time suddenly appear as one point of light in an infinite mesh of light.

Yet even after we had taken this step, we would still not have attained the stage of *caritas* and *agape* in the strict sense. The true motives of that remarkable nun in Calcutta would not yet have come into view. Incidentally, when a reporter remarked to her in astonishment that he would not do "anything like that" if he were paid a thousand dollars a day for it, she is said to have replied, tersely and magnificently, "Neither would I." Anyone who seriously asked her, "Why are you doing this?" would probably receive the reply — if she did not choose to remain silent — "For the sake of Christ!" At this point Anders Nygren is undeniably right; love in the form of agape is "the original basic conception of Christianity."[8] It rests upon the certain faith that the event which in the language of theology is called "Incarnation" conferred upon man the gift of an immediate and real participation in God's creative power of affirmation. Or as we might also put it: participation in the divine love, which is what creates the being as well as the goodness of the world in the first place. As a consequence of that man can turn to another person in a way that otherwise he would be utterly incapable of doing and, while remaining altogether himself, can say to that other, "It's good that you are." And it is precisely this more intensive force of approval, operating from a wholly fresh basis, that is intended by the word *caritas* (*agape*). But because like God's own love it is universal, at least in intention, excluding nothing and no one, we find we can use the word meaningfully without explicitly naming an object, saying for example that someone is "in love" (1 Jn 4:18). Such love, no matter how "forlorn"[9] it may seem, possesses that imperturbable non-irritability of which the New Testament speaks: *caritas non irritatur* (1 Cor 13:5). Likewise other hyperboles, such as that in love a maximum of freedom is attained[10] and that it gives the heart perfect peace,[11] prove true only with regard to *caritas*.

It is really self-evident that the images hitherto employed, of a succession of steps and stages, do not quite accord with the radical newness and otherness of that participation in the creative love of God which has been given to man — what in the New Testament is called Grace. Nevertheless, the great tradition of Christendom has always insisted that this new thing is indeed tied to what man is by nature and by virtue of creation with an inseparable, though almost indescribable, bond.

Above all, *caritas* in the Christian sense does not invalidate any of the love and affirmation which we are able to feel on our own, and which frequently we do feel as a matter of course. Rather, *caritas* comprehends all the forms of human love.[12] For after all it is our own natural, native will, kindled at the Creation and by virtue of this very origin tempestuously demanding appeasement, that is now exalted to immediate participation in the will of the Creator Himself — and therefore necessarily presupposed.[13]

Anyone who considers and accepts this principle cannot find it surprising that the whole conception of *caritas* is dominated by felicity. If happiness is truly never anything but happiness in love, then the fruit of that highest form of love must be the utmost happiness, for which language offers such names as felicity, beatitude, bliss. Nor should this be in any way confused with "eudemonism." In the first place felicity means not so much the subjective feeling of happiness as the objective, existential appeasement of the will by the *bonum universale*,[14] by the quintessence of everything for which our whole being hungers and which we are capable of longing for in (only seemingly paradoxical) "selfless self-love." Moreover, felicity, as has already been said, cannot be defined positively at all in regard to its content; it is a *bonum ineffabile*,[15] toward which our love ultimately directs itself, a good that cannot be grasped in words.

At any rate, although we may find the fact startling and troublesome at first, the great teachers of Christendom always considered the concepts of *caritas* and felicity as very closely linked. "*Caritas* is not just any kind of love of God, but a love for God that loves him as the object and the author of happiness."[16] And in the world, we are told, we can love in the mode of *caritas* only what is capable of sharing happiness, or beatitude, with us.[17] This includes our bodies, into which happiness will "flood back";[18] but above all our fellow men, insofar as they will be our companions in beatitude[19] (or ought to be[20]).

Of course it is possible to ask skeptically just what it means to love another as the possible companion of future beatitude. Would love of this sort alter matters at all? I think that in fact a great deal would be altered if we succeeded in regarding another person (whether friend, beloved, son, neighbor, adversary and rival or even an unknown who needed our help) truly as one destined like ourselves to share in the perfection of bliss, as our *socius in participatione beatudinis*.[21] That other person would then, in my view, simply enter into a new dimension of reality. From one moment to the next we would realize that "there are no ordinary people."[22]

It is no accident that almost all the above has been written in the conditional tense, the *modus irrealis*. In fact it happens very seldom, and only to a few persons, to see the extra-ordinariness of everyone ("wonderfully created and even more wonderfully re-created"[23]), let alone to respond to it with the exclamation of love: It's wonderful that you are! This is, as we see, not so very far from the vocabulary of eros. And truly, if anyone has asked what in the world the mutual rapture of lovers has to do with the work of a nun who wishes to succor dying beggars — precisely this is the point at which the hidden common element becomes visible, as if seen through a tiny crack.

It also becomes immediately apparent that the act of *caritas* is not simply a further step on the road of eros, and that what is involved is something different from mere "sublimation." It is true that *caritas* can be incorporated into the most commonplace forms of expression in men's dealings with their fellows. In fact, that is usually what will be done with it — so that possibly, to the uninitiated eye, there will be scarcely anything noticeable about its outward appearance to set it off from the usual conduct of people reasonably well-disposed toward one another. In other words, the natural forms of love are presupposed to be intact; and no special, solemnly sublime vocabulary is needed to describe the operations of *caritas*. Still, the classical statement of the relationship of Grace and Nature speaks not only of presupposition and intactness, but also of the perfecting of what man by nature is and has.[24] And when I said that the bond between eros and *caritas* exists but is almost indescribable, the difficulty of description in practice consists in this question: "What is the meaning of "perfecting"? This is one of those concepts which probably can never be known and defined before it is experienced. It is simply in the nature of the thing that the apprentice can have no specific idea of what the perfection of mastery looks like from inside, and all that is going to demand of him. Perfection always includes transformation. And transformation necessarily means parting from what must be overcome and abandoned precisely for the sake of preserving identity in change.

"Perfection" in *caritas*, therefore, may very well mean that eros, in order to keep its original impulse and remain really love, above all in order to attain the "foreverness" that it naturally desires, must transform itself altogether, and that this transformation perhaps resembles passing through something akin to dying. Such thoughts are, at any rate, not unfamiliar to mankind's reflections on love. *Caritas*, in renewing and rejuvenating us, also brings us death in a certain sense: *facit in nobis quamdam mortem*, says Augustine.[25] The same thing is conveyed by the familiar figure of speech which calls *caritas*, because it consumes everything and transforms everything into itself, a fire.[26]

Thus it is much more than an innocuous piety when Christendom prays, "Kindle in us the fire of Thy love."

NOTES

In the following notes quotations from St. Thomas Aquinas's *Summa theologica* are indicated only by numerals. (For example, "I, II, 3, 4" means, "Part I of Section II, quaestio 3, articulus 4.") The same method is used for references to his commentary on the *Sentences* of Peter Lombard. (For example, "2 d. 3, 4, 1" means, "Book 2, distinctio 3, quaestio 4, articulus 1."). The titles of the other works of St. Thomas are abbreviated as follows:

C.G.	*Summa contra Gentes*
Pot.	*Quaestiones disputatae de potentia Dei*
Car.	*Quaestio disputata de caritate*
De spe	*Quaestio disputata de spe*
Quol.	*Quaesitones quodlibetales*
Perf. vit. spir.	*De perfectione vitae spiritualis*
In Div. Nom.	*Commentary on Dionysius Areopagita's De divinis nominibus*
In Isa.	*Commentary on Isaiah*

The motto is taken from Thomas Aquinas's *Summa theologica* (I, 38, 2): *Amor habet rationem primi doni, per quod omnia dona gratuita donantur.*

I

[1] This accurate expression comes from Theodor W. Adorno's *Noten zur Literatur,* vol. II (Frankfurt, 1961), p. 7.

[2] Ulrich von Wilamowitz-Moellendorff. Anders Nygren used the phrase quoted here as a motto in his two-volume work, *Eros und Agape* (Gütersloh, 1930, 1937), vol. I, p. 43.

[3] Johannes Rehmke, *Grundlegung der Ethik als Wissenschaft* (Leipzig, 1925), pp. 98 f., 114.

[4] I, II, 26, 3.

[5] Gesammelte Werke (London, 1940 ff.), vol. XIV, 462.

[6] *Ibid.,* vol. XIII, 122.

[7] *Ainsi soit-il ou les jeux sont faits* (Paris, 1952), p. 156.

[8] *Studies in Words* (Cambridge, 1967), p. 173.

[9] Hermann Paul, *Deutsches Wörterbuch,* 4th ed., revised by Karl Euling (Halle, 1935), p. 353.

[10] "Constant love is called *Minne*" — Ulrich von Lichtenstein. Cf. *Trübners Deutsches Wörterbuch,* vol. IV (Berlin, 1943), p. 631.

[11] Vol. VI, col. 2239 f.

[12] Cf. Fr. von Lipperheide, *Spruchwörterbuch* (Berlin, 1962), p. 620.

[13] Kluge-Götze, *Etymologisches Wörterbuch der deutschen Sprache,* 11th ed. (Berlin, 1934), p. 392.

[14] *Trübners Deutsches Wörterbuch,* vol. IV, p. 631.

[15] Ibid., vol. IV, p. 632.

[16] Vol. VI, col. 2241.

[17] Düsseldorf-Cologne, 1956 ff.

[18] The word *Karitas* first appears in the "Duden" in the ninth edition of 1915; the spelling with *K* is indicated as preferred, although *Caritas* is also mentioned. This spelling was consistently used up to the 16th edition of 1967. Karl Jaspers in his *Philosophie* also speaks exclusively of *Karitas.*

[19] Karl Jaspers, *Philosophie,* 2nd ed. (Berlin, 1948), pp. 623 ff.

[20] *City of God* 10, 1.

[21] Carl Abel, *Über den Begriff der Liebe in einigen alten und neuen Sprachen* (Berlin, 1872), p. 11. The well-known phrase from Tacitus (Annals I, 1), *sine ira et studio,* likewise means approximately: without anger and *predilection.* And when Sallust (*De coniuratione Catilinae*) says that the powerful man may neither love nor hate, he too uses the word *studere* (*neque studere neque odisse*).

[22] *Sämtliche Werke* (Insel-Ausgabe) (Leipzig, n.d.), vol. I, 493.

[23] Goethe in a letter dated January 2, 1800 to F. H. Jacobi, ". . . that true appreciation cannot be without mercifulness."

[24] To Riemer on July 11, 1810.

[25] 3 d. 27, 2, 1.

[26] Thomas Aquinas says that what the concept of *caritas* adds to that of *amor* is, as the word itself indicates, the appreciation of superior value (I, II, 26, 3).

[27] In Cicero, for example, we find the phrase *caritas generis humani* (*De finibus bonorum et malorum* 5, 23, 65). Cf. also *Partitiones oratoriae* 16, 56 and 25, 88.

[28] François de Sales, *Traité de l'amour de Dieu,* vol. I (Annecy, 1894), p. 73.

[29] *In Epistolam Johannis ad Parthos tractatus* 8, 5. Migne, *Patrologia Latina* 35, 2098.

[30] *City of God* 14, 7. Cf. also *D Trinitate* 15, 18; 32.

[31] Cf. for example Jn 15:9; 16:27; Rom 5:5; 2 Pt 1:7.

[32] *Aias* 693. I owe this reference to the Greek-English dictionary of Liddell and Scott (Oxford, 1958), p. 695.

[33] Sophocles, *Antigone* 523: *symphilein éphyn.*

[34] *Kirchliche Dogmatik,* IV, 2 (Zollikon-Zürich, 1955), p. 836.

[35] Quoted in Heinrich Scholz, *Eros und Caritas. Die platonische Liebe und die Liebe im Sinne des Christentums* (Halle, 1929), p. 112.

[36] *Philadelphia:* Rom 12:10; 1 Thes 4:95; Heb 13:1; 2 Pt 1:7. *Philanthropia:* Ti 3:4.

[37] Rollo May, *Love and Will* (New York, 1969), p. 73.

[38] Ibid., p. 65.

[39] C. S. Lewis, *The Four Loves* (London, 1960), p. 19.

[40] C. T. Lewis and C. Short, *A Latin Dictionary* (Oxford, 1958), p. 107.

[41] In the Polish-German border region there is (or was) a remarkable colloquial phrase which corroborates this assumption. The phrase is (or was): "Das ist sehr gleich" — literally: "That is very like." The meaning: "That is true and I like it." Cf. C. Abel, *Der Begriff der Liebe*, p. 42, n.

[42] *Love, Power, Justice* (New York, 1954), p. 25.

[43] Abel, *Begriff der Liebe*, p. 17.

[44] *The Century Dictionary and Cyclopedia* (New York, 1911), vol. VIII, p. 4963.

[45] Cf., say, Littré's *Dictionnaire de la langue Française,* 1956 edition.

[46] Abel, *Begriff der Liebe*, p. 31.

[47] *Confessions* 4, 13; *On Music* 6, 13.

[48] The German word *schön* (beautiful) is connected with *schauen* (to see); its literal meaning is "worth seeing."

[49] This would greatly distinguish them from the Greeks. Plato, at any rate, expressed the conviction that the world and man sprang from the goodness of the Creator, who was without jealousy. Cf. *Timaeus* 29 d.

[50] I owe this information to my colleague Professor Hubert Rösel.

II

[1] Johannes Hoffmeister, *Wörterbuch der philosophischen* (Hamburg, 1955), p. 670.

[2] Cf. Josef Pieper, *Leisure the Basis of Culture,* revised ed. (New York, 1964), p. 9 ff.; *Happiness and Contemplation* (New York, 1958), pp. 74, 80.

[3] Dietrich von Hildebrand, *Transformation in Christ,* (New York, 1948), p. 96.

[4] Paul Ricoeur, *Philosophie de la volonté,* vol. I (Paris, 1963), p. 322.

[5] Pot. 3, 15 ad 14.

[6] *Somme théologique.* La Charité I (Paris, 1967), pp. 277 f.

[7] For example: Ps 22:9; 41:12.

[8] This has recently been included in the German edition of the Jerusalem Bible (Freiburg, 1968).

[9] *Primus . . . motus voluntatis et cuiuslibet appetitivae virtutis est amor.* I, 20, 1.

[10] *Omnis actus appetitivae virtutis ex amore seu dilectione derivatur.* I, 60 prologue. Cf. also I, 20, 1: C.G. 4, 19.

[11] Car. 21 . . . *principium omnium voluntiarum affectionum.*

[12] Augustine, *City of God* 14, 6.

[13] Thomas Aquinas II, II, 34, 4.

[14] *Talis est quisque, qualis eius dilectio.* Augustine, *In Epistolam Johannis ad Parthos* 2, 14. Migne, *Patrologia Latina* 35, 1997.

[15] Augustine, *Contra Faustum* 5, 10. Migne, Patrologia Latina 42, 228.

[16] *City of God* 15, 22.

[17] *Primo vult suum amicum esse et vivere.* II, II, 25, 7. Thomas does not even shrink from the conclusion that this assent of the will extends, for one who loves out of supernatural *caritas,* even to the demons, to the fallen angels! We want (*volumus*) he writes in the same *Summa Theologica* — in the treatise on *caritas* — that those spirits may be sustained and preserved in what they are by nature (II, II, 25, 11).

[18] Maurice Nédoncelle, *Vers une philosophie de l'amour et de la personne* (Paris, 1957), p. 15.

[19] "Zur Psychologie der Gesinnungen." *Jahrbuch fur Philosophie und phänomenologische Forschung,* Jg. 1 (1925), p. 368.

[20] *Ibid.,* p. 370.

[21] *Ibid,* p, 369.

[22] *On Love* (New York, 1957), p. 20.

[23] *Ibid.*

[24] *Exigences philosophiques du Christianisme* (Paris, 1950), p. 241.

[25] *Deutsche Gesamtausgabe der Werke von Vladimir Solowjew,* Wl. Szylkarski, ed., vol. VII (Munich, 1953).

[26] *Geheimnis des Seins* (Vienna, 1952), p. 472.

[27] Pfänder, *Psychologie der Gesinnungen,* p. 368.

[28] *Sinn der Geschlechterliebe,* p. 235.

[29] *Also sprach Zarathustra* I. *Gesammelte Werke,* Musarion-Ausgabe (Munich, 1922), vol. 13, p. 46.

[30] Etienne Gilson, *History of Christian Philosophy in the Middle Ages* (London, 1955), p. 83.

[31] In an interview in the weekly *Action* (December 29, 1944). Cf. also *L'Existentialisme est un humanisme* (Paris, 1946), p. 18.

[32] Georg Simmel, *Fragmente und Aufsätze* (Munich, 1923), p. 24.

[33] *Amor Dei est infundens et creans bonitatem in rebus.* I, 20, 2.

III

[1] *Being and Nothingness* (New York, 1956), p. 371.

[2] "Hospitalism." In *The Psychoanalytic Study of the Child* I (London, 1945).

[3] *The Art of Loving* (New York, 1952).

[4] The cover of the American pocket book edition (Bantam Books, New York) speaks of "the world-famous psychiatrist's *daring* prescription for love."

[5] *Ibid.,* p. 41 f.

[6] *Ibid.,* p. 42.

[7] Robert O. Johann, *Building the Human* (New York, 1968), p. 161.

[8] Frederick D. Wilhelmsen, *The Metaphysics of Love* (New York, 1962), p. 139.

[9] Karl Marx in his youth used this very phrase. Cf. Karl Marx,

Texte zu Methode und Praxis II. Rowohlts Klassiker (Hamburg, 1968), p. 180.

[10] *The Art of Loving,* p. 41.

[11] Cf. *L'existentialisme est un humanisme,* pp. 21 ff.

[12] Book 13, chap. 38.

[13] *Deus proprie loquendo neminem amat. Ethica* V, propos. 17, corollarium.

[14] Ladislaus Grünhut, *Eros und Agape. Eine metaphysisch-religions-philosophische Untersuchung.* (Leipzig, 1931), p. 20.

[15] Mt 6:22.

[16] This is the Jesuit Stanislaus, Count of Dunin-Borkowski (1864–1934), known to scholarship chiefly by his work in several volumes on Spinoza (Münster 1910–1936).

[17] Sartre, for example, interprets the idea that God "determined Adam's nature" as something in itself incompatible with human freedom. *L'Etre et le Néant,* p. 622.

[18] *Menschliches, Allzumenschliches* I, No. 603.

[19] C. S. Lewis, *The Four Loves,* p. 150.

[20] *Ibid.*

[21] *Symposium* 178 d-179 a.

[22] Cf. II, II, 75, 1; 75 1 ad 3.

[23] *Ubi amor, ibi oculus.* This maxim by Richard of St. Victor (Benjamin Minor, cap. 13) is also cited by Thomas Aquinas, for example in the *Commentary on the Sentences* (3 d. 35, 1, 2, 1).

[24] Nicolai Hartmann, *Ethik,* 3rd ed. (Berlin, 1949), p. 538.

[25] *Ibid.* Franz von Baader also speaks of "that natural phantasmagoria as a consequence of which lovers mutually seem more beautiful, more lovable, more perfect and better than they are; but he adds realistically that the lovers ought to "take this rapture . . . only as an encouraging summons." *Sätze aus der erotischen Philosophie* (1828). Republished under the same title, ed. G.-K. Kaltenbrunner, Sammlung Insel (Frankfurt, 1966), p. 109.

[26] *Menschliches, Allzumenschliches* I, No. 523.

[27] Fromm, *The Art of Loving,* p. 1.

[28] *Gesammelte Werke* (Suhrkamp Verlag) (Frankfurt, 1967), vol. XII, p. 407.

[29] *Symposium* 180 b.

[30] *Gesammelte Werke,* vol. XIV, p. 492.

[31] *Ibid.,* p. 484.

[32] *Ibid.,* p. 487.

[33] *Ibid.,* p. 486.

[34] *Ibid.,* p. 489 f.

[35] *Theologisches Wörterbuch zum Neven Testament,* vol. II, p. 738.

[36] Augustine, *Contra Maximinum* 2, 13. Migne, *Patrologia Latina* 42, 770; similarly, 40, 22.

IV

[1] C. S. Lewis, *The Problem of Pain* (New York: The Macmillan Company, 17th printing, 1967), p. 34.

[2] *In epistolam Johannis ad Parthos* 7, 8. Migne, *Patrologia Latina* 35, 2033.

[3] *Sermones de tempore* 49, 4. Migne, *Patrologia Latina* 38, 322.

[4] C. S. Lewis, *The Problem of Pain,* p. 29.

[5] *Ibid.,* p. 31.

[6] Georges Bernanos,

[7] "If you are without chastening, then you are bastards and not sons." Heb 12:8.

[8] II, II, 25, 1.

[9] 1 Cor 13.

[10] *Der Mut zum Sein* (Stuttgardt, 1954).

[11] *Ibid.,* p. 131.

[12] II, II, 27, 2; obj. 1.

[13] 2, 4; 80 b.

[14] "What else does it mean to love someone, if not that we wish him to receive the greatest goods?" Cicero, *De finibus bonorum et malorum* 2, 24, 78.

[15] II, II, 27, 2.

[16] Incidentally, Aristotle himself said almost the same thing in the *Nicomachean Ethics* (9, 5; 1166 b).

[17] *On Death and Dying* (New York, 1969).

[18] *Ibid.,* p. 8.

[19] II, II, 27, 2.

[20] *Psychologie der Gesinnungen,* p. 370.

[21] I, II, 67, 5 ad 3. Thomas is here quoting Aristotle (*Nicomachean Ethics* 9, 5; 1167 a).

[22] *Sämtliche Werke* (Insel-Ausgabe) (Leipzig, n.d.), vol. II, pp. 1328 f.

[23] Robert G. Hazo, *The Idea of Love* (New York, 1967).

[24] *Ibid.,* p. 39.

[25] *Gesammelte Werke,* vol. XIV, p. 461.

[26] *Die Laune des Verliebten,* scene 5.

[27] *Vita nuova,* chap. 11.

[28] Cf. Josef Pieper, *Missbrauch der Sprache, Missbrauch der Macht* (Zurich, 1970), pp. 36 f.

[29] I, 109, 1 ad 1.

[30] The Poems of Catullus. Translated by Horace Gregory (New York, 1956), p. 151.

[31] Cf. also I, II, 28, 4.

[32] *Gesammelte Werke,* vol. XIV, p. 461.

[33] Gabriel Madinier, *Conscience et amour,* 2nd ed. (Paris, 1947), p. 95.

[34] Robert O. Johann, *The Meaning of Love* (Glen Rock, N.J., 1966), p. 26.

[35] Wilhelmsen, *The Metaphysics of Love,* p. 37.

[36] *Eros und Liebe* (Berlin, 1937), p. 26.

[37] Though the fine saying attributed to Rousseau ought to be considered: One contemplates the beloved, but does not scrutinize him.

[38] *Eros und Liebe,* p. 26.

V

[1] *Nicomachean Ethics* 8, 2; 1155 b.

[2] Cf. C. S. Lewis, *The Four Loves* (London, 1960), p. 23.

[3] II, II, 141, 4 ad 3. Cf. also Mal. 8, 1 ad 9.

[4] Cf. Josef Pieper, *The Four Cardinal Virtues* (New York, 1965), pp. 166 f.

[5] *In Epistolam Johannis ad Parthos* 8, 5. Migne, *Patrologia Latina* 35, 2058.

[6] *Symposium* 189 f.

[7] Hazo, *Idea of Love,* p. 160.

[8] This distinction between need-love and gift-love restates the well-known antithesis between *amor concupiscentiae* and *amor benevolentiae* (*amor amicitiae*), between desirous love and the well-wishing love between friends. As far as the subject goes, the distinction is probably as old as human reflection on the subject of love; and the terms, too, have been part of the textbook vocabularies in philosophy and theology for many centuries. Thomas Aquinas likewise employs this terminology, but at the same time he seems to hint at a slight aloofness from it. He himself apparently prefers to speak of "imperfect" and "perfect" love (e.g., *De Spe* 3). But despite appearances he expressly does not intend these terms to be evaluative, at least not in any moral sense. Rather, in a purely descriptive way, he means: if we "love" to drink wine for a festive meal, obviously this "desirous" love directed toward the wine is imperfect insofar as the wine is not at all what is primarily and really loved. The real object of our love is we ourselves; and understood in this sense the love directed toward ourselves is "perfect"; which means nothing more nor less than that the concept of "love" is realized in its full, un-unweakened sense. Normally, however, as indicated above, Thomas adopts the usual terminology, but qualifies it by saying that it is proposed or used *a quibusdam,* by certain writers (I, 60, 3).

[9] *The Four Loves,* pp. 10 f.

[10] Heinrich Scholz, *Eros und Caritas. Die platonische Liebe und die Liebe im Sinne des Christentums* (Halle, 1929). Anders Nygren, *Eros und Agape. Gestaltwandlungen der christlichen Liebe.* Two vols. (Gütersloh, 1930, 1937). Emil Brunner, *Eros und Liebe* (Berlin, 1937).

[11] Heinrich Scholz is better known for his later writings on philosophy and logic; but he began his university career with a dissertation on the philosophy of religion and systematic philosophy (under Adolf von Harnack).

[12] Nygren is regarded as one of the leading figures in modern Protestant theology. Professor at the University of Lund, later Bishop of Lund, he served from 1947 to 1952 as first president of the Lutheran World Federation. His principal work is *Eros und Agape.*

[13] *Eros und Agape* I, p. 31.

[14] *Ibid.*

[15] *Ibid.*, pp. 185 f.

[16] *Ibid.* II, p. 12.

[17] *Ibid.* I, p. 192.

[18] *Ibid.* II, p. 533.

[19] *Ibid.* II, p. 548.

[20] *Ibid.* II, p. 549.

[21] *Ibid.* I, p. 56; II, p. 549.

[22] *Ibid.* II, p. 551.

[23] *Ibid.* I, p. 60.

[24] *Ibid.* II, p. 548.

[25] *Ibid.* II, p. 551.

[26] *Ibid.* I, pp. 185 f.

[27] *Ibid.* I, p. 60.

[28] *Ibid.* I, pp. 185 f.

[29] *Ibid.*

[30] *Ibid.* II, p. 11.

[31] *Ibid.*

[32] *Ibid.* I, p. 192.

[33] *Ibid.* I, p. 154.

[34] Confessions I, 1.

[35] *Eros und Agape* II, p. 297.

[36] *Ibid.* I, p. 35.

[37] *Ibid.* II, pp. 472 f.

[38] *Ibid.* II, pp. 244 ff.

[39] *Ibid.* II, p. 255.

[40] *Ibid.* II, p. 465.

[41] *Ibid.* II, p. 467.

[42] *Ibid.* II, p. 255.

[43] *Ibid.* II, p. 378.

[44] *Ibid.* II, p. 544.

[45] *Ibid.* I, p. 40.

[46] *Ibid.* II, p. 561.

[47] *Karl Barth. Darstellung und Deutung seiner Theologie* (Cologne, 1951), pp. 35 f.

[48] *Kirchliche Dogmatik,* vol. III, part 4 (Zollikon-Zurich, 1951), p. 241.

[49] This is done in vol. IV (part 2) of the *Kirchliche Dogmatik,* in a chapter headed "The Problem of Christian Love" (pp. 825 ff.).

[50] *Kirchliche Dogmatik* IV, 2, pp. 834, 837.

[51] *Ibid.*, pp. 836 f.

[52] *Ibid.*, p. 837.

[53] *Ibid.*, pp. 833 f.

[54] *Ibid.* p. 833; p. 845.

[55] *Ibid.* p. 844.

[56] *Ibid.* p. 833.

[57] *Ibid.* p. 835.

[58] *Ibid.* p. 834.

[59] *Ibid.*

[60] *Eros und Agape* II, p. 557.

[61] Grünhut, *Eros und Agape*, pp. 20 f.

[62] Erwin Reissner, *Glaube, Hoffnung, Liebe* (Hamburg, 1954), p. 44.

[63] C. S. Lewis, *The Four Loves*, p. 11.

[64] G. Simmel, *Fragmente und Aufsätze*, p. 14.

VI

[1] *Eros und Agape* II, p. 110.

[2] *Ibid.* II, pp. 464 f.

[3] *Dato enim, per impossibile, quod Deus non esset hominis bonum, non esset ei ratio diligendi.* II, II, 26, 13 ad 3.

[4] In fact the *articulus* of the *Summa theologica* (II, II, 26, 13) from which this proposition comes bears the heading: "Whether the order of love remains valid in the Eternal Life?" (*Utrum ordo caritatis remaneat in patria*).

[5] C. S. Lewis, *The Four Loves*, p. 12.

[6] *Ibid.* p. 11.

[7] Cf. Joseph Pieper, *The Four Cardinal Virtues*, pp. 147 f.

[8] *Pondus meum amor meus; eo feror, quocumque feror. Confessions* 13, 9.

[9] *Nihil habet dominium suae naturae.* I, 60, 1, obj. 2.

[10] I, 60, 3.

[11] Kirchliche Dogmatik IV, 2, p. 835.

[12] C. G. 4, 92.

[13] Harvey Cox, *The Secular City* (New York: Macmillan, 1965), p. 96.

[14] In *Man and his Future*, ed. G. Wolstenholme (London, 1963), p. 12.

[15] *City of God* 11, 27. Still it must be considered that *in concreto* the boundaries between "genuine" justified happiness and a merely "caused" feeling of happiness are fluid. When we read in th Psalter (Ps 104:15): "Wine gladdens the heart of man," is not the reference to what may crudely be termed a chemically and physiologically caused "gladness"? I would comment: It depends whether what is involved is a heightening of an already joyous and festive hour, or an artificial and deliberate substitute for gladness. Still, in Pascal's treatise on the passions there is the remarkable and, to my mind, rather dubious sentence: "What

does it matter whether a joy is false if we are convinced that it is true?"

[16] Cf. Helmut Gollwitzer, . . . und führen, wohin du nicht willst (Munich, 1951).

[17] Rollo May, Love and Will, p. 27. In the same book (p. 111) may be found the sentence: "The most tragic of all, in the long run, is the ultimate attitude, 'It doesn't matter.'"

[18] Ibid., p. 29.

[19] Carl Zuckmayer, A Part of Myself, tr. by Richard and Clara Winston (New York, 1970), p. 396. The words "not to have to hate" are emphasized by italics in the original.

[20] Gesammelte Werke, vol. XIV, p. 441.

[21] Rollo May, Love and Will, p. 102.

[22] Sine dolore non vivitur in amore. Quoted from J. Guitton, Vom Wesen der Liebe zwischen Mann und Frau (Freiburg, 1960), p. 168.

[23] The Four Loves, p. 138.

[24] II, II, 28, 1.

[25] C. S. Lewis, The Screwtape Letters (London: Fontana Books, 1969), p. 92.

[26] Amor est laetitia concomitante idea causae externae. Ethica III (Definitiones); also Ethica IV, propos. 44.

[27] Psychologie der Gesinnungen, p. 357.

[28] Ibid., p. 355.

[29] Sämtliche Werke II, p. 1325.

[30] This is true for quite a few "definitions" that may be found in philosophical writing. Here are only two examples: "The true essence of love consists in abandoning consciousness of oneself, forgetting oneself in another self, and yet for the first time having and possessing oneself in this fading and forgetting." Thus Hegel in his Aesthetik (vol. I, 2nd ed., [Frankfurt 1955]), p. 519. In this characterization, grandly impressive though it is, the "transitive" nature of love and "the other" scarcely appear. Still less do they in the following definition by Max Scheler, which holds that love is "the intentional movement in which from a given value A of an object the phenomenon of a higher value is attained" (Wesen und Formen der Sympathie [Frankfurt, 1948]), p. 177; or that it is "a movement which proceeds from the lower to the higher value and in which any given higher value of an objcet or a person first flashes into being" (ibid.). In such descriptions the simple fact of love familiar to everyone is scarcely recognizable.

[31] Amare sive diligere est felicitate alterius delectari. Opera Omnia (ed. L. Dutens), vol. IV, 3, p. 295.

[32] Neue Abhandlungen über den menschlichen Verstand. In G. W. Leibniz, Philosophische Schriften. Ed. W. v. Engelhardt and H. H. Holz. Vol. III, 1 (Darmstadt, 1959), pp. 224 f.

[33] Vol. I, p. 71.

[34] *Kritik der praktischen Vernunft.* In *Werke,* ed. W. Weischedel, vol. IV (Wiesbaden, 1956), p. 208.

[35] *Ibid.,* vol. VI (Frankfurt, 1964), p. 138.

[36] *Ibid.* vol. IV, p. 205.

VII

[1] I, 94, 1.

[2] I, 19, 10.

[3] I, II, 10, 2.

[4] "Man is a needy being insofar as he belongs to the sensual world." Kant, *Kritik der praktischen Vernunft* (I, 1, 2), *Werke,* vol. IV, p. 179.

[5] *Nicomachean Ethics* 9, 4; 1166 a.

[6] *Ibid.* 9, 4; 1166 b.

[7] I, II, 2, 7 ad 2.

[8] 3 d. 28, 1, 6: derivatur.

[9] *Ibid.*

[10] II, II, 25, 4. Similarly: 3 d. 29, 1, 3 ad 3; C.G. 3, 153; Quol. 5, 6; Car. 7 ad 11.

[11] *Dictionnaire Philosophique,* article Amour-Propre. *Oeuvres Complètes* (Paris, 1825), vol. 51, p. 326.

[12] I, II, 27, 3.

[13] Cf. II, II, 25, 4.

[14] Cf. Josef Pieper, *Guide to Thomas Aquinas* (New York, 1962), pp. 43 ff.

[15] Serm. 368, 5. Migne, Patrologia Latina 39, 1655.

[16] *City of God* 1, 20.

[17] Martin C. d'Arcy, *The Mind and Heart of Love* (London, 1945), pp. 323, 325.

[18] 9, 4; 1166 a.

[19] *Christian Behaviour* (London, 1943), pp. 38 f.

[20] *Quod non propter se amatur, non amatur. Soliloquia* 1, 13. Migne, *Patrologia Latina* 32, 881.

[21] *Si amas, gratis ama.* Serm. 165, 4. Migne, *Patrologia Latina* 38, 905.

[22] *Ecce Homo.* Gesammelte Werke, Musarion-Ausgabe (Munich, 1922 ff.), vol. 21, p. 220.

[23] *Ibid.,* vol. 11, p. 221.

[24] *Ibid.*

[25] *Menschliches, Allzumenschliches* II, 95. *Gesammelte Werke,* vol. 9, p. 58.

[26] 192 c—d.

[27] *Omnes . . . per beatitudinem intelligunt quemdam perfectissimum statum; sed in quo consistat ille status perfectus . . . occultum est.* 2 d 38, 1, 2 ad 2.

[28] *Das Prinzip Hoffnung* (Frankfurt, 1959), p. 221.

[29] To Sara von Grotthuss on April 23, 1814.

[30] *Opera Omnia,* vol. IV, 3, p. 295.
[31] *Eros und Agape* II, p. 110.
[32] Serm. 165, 4. Migne, Patrologia Latina 38, 905.
[33] *Enarrationes in Psalmos* 118, 22, 2. Migne, *Patrologia Latina* 37, 1563.
[34] Cf. C. S. Lewis, *The Problem of Pain,* p. 64.
[35] *De diligendo Deo.* Ed. W. W. Wiliams (Cambridge, 1926), pp. 32 f.
[36] Serm. 368, 1. Migne, *Patrologia Latina* 39, 1652. In the same sermon (cap. 5) there is the formulation: "Whoso loves his soul will lose it because he loves it. You do not want to lose it? Then you are incapable of not loving it."

VIII

[1] *De divinis nominibus* 15, 180. Cf. also Thomas Aquinas, In Div. Nom. 4, 12; No. 455.
[2] II, II, 17, 3.
[3] Jules Michelet, *L'amour,* 4th ed. (Paris, 1859), p. 398. Similarly, Erich Fromm, *Art of Loving,* p. 17.
[4] C. S. Lewis, *The Screwtape Letters,* p. 92.
[5] Ernst Bloch, *Erbschaft dieser Zeit* (Frankfurt, 1962), p. 157.
[6] *Unio est consequens amorem.* I, II, 26, 2 ad 2.
[7] *On Love,* p. 51.
[8] *Eine Vorlesung Kants über Ethik,* ed. Paul Menzer (Berlin, 1925), pp. 204 f.
[9] Munich, 1941, p. 251.
[10] *Symposium* 202c.
[11] *On Love,* p. 51.
[12] *Campagne in Frankreich,* Münster, Dec. 1792.
[13] Paul Claudel, *The City,* end of Act Three.
[14] The Four Loves, p. 131. Similarly in *They Asked for a Paper* (London, 1962), p. 200.
[15] Freud calls all non-sexual love "goal-inhibited love"; it "was originally fully sensual love and still is in the person's unconscious." *Gesammelte Werke,* vol. XIV, p. 462.
[16] *Love and Will,* p. 76.
[17] Part I, Book 5.
[18] *Phaedrus* 256.
[19] *Ibid.,* 256 b 3.
[20] Paul Claudel/Jacques Rivière, *Correspondance 1907–1914.*
[21] *Phaedrus* 256 e 4.
[22] Cf. Josef Pieper, *Enthusiasm and Divine Madness. On the Platonic Dialogue* Phaedrus (New York, 1964), pp. 95 f.
[23] George Santayana, "Friendship." In *The Birth of Reason and other essays,* ed. D. Gory (New York, 1968), p. 83.
[24] C. S. Lewis, *The Four Loves,* p. 130.
[25] *Dichtergehäuse* (Zurich-Munich, 1966), p. 40.
[26] Quoted in Jean Guitton, *Vom Wesen der Liebe zwischen Mann und Frau,* p. 313.

[27] Cf. C. S. Lewis, *The Four Loves*, p. 131.
[28] R. W. Emerson, *Essays* (first series) (London, 1903), p. 128.
[29] *Fragmente und Aufsätze*, p. 9.
[30] Thus in the book *On the Divine Names* (4, 12; 164). But like so much in the history of Dionysius Areopagita's influence (on this subject cf. Josef Pieper, *Scholasticism* [New York, 1960], pp. 46 ff.) this idea also rests upon a misunderstanding, specifically upon misinterpretation of a sentence in the Epistle to the Romans of Ignatius of Antioch. There it is stated (7, 2): "My love (*eros*) is crucified." Dionysius, as Origen had done before him, understands this to mean that Christ is referred to in the sense of eros, beloved. But the context clearly shows that what is meant is: my erotic love (for worldly things) has been nailed to the cross with Christ. Long before Anders Nygren (*Eros und Agape* II, pp. 409 ff.), Fr. X. Funk pointed this out as early as 1901 in his edition of the Apostolic Fathers (*Patres Apostolici*, vol. I (Tübingen, 1901), p. 261.
[31] I, II, 26, 3 ad 4.
[32] *Traité de l'amour de Dieu*, vol. I, p. 53.
[33] *Le nom de l'amour, comme plus excellent, a été justement donné à la charité. Ibid.*, p. 73.
[34] *Kirchliche Dogmatik* III, 4, p. 140.
[35] *Religion und Eros*, p. 123.
[36] *Ibid.*, p. 278.
[37] *Ibid.*, p. 123.
[38] *Kirchliche Dogmatik* III, 4, p. 134.
[39] *Ibid.*, pp. 135 f.
[40] Cf. C. S. Lewis, *The Four Loves*, p. 130.
[41] *Ibid.*, p. 128.
[42] *Ibid.*, p. 17.
[43] *De amore sponsi ad sponsam.*

IX

[1] Translated from the German translation by Otto Karrer, *New Testament* (Munich, 1959).
[2] I, 60, 5.
[3] Cf. Josef Pieper, "Was heisst 'Christliches Abendland'?" In *Tradition als Herausforderung. Aufsätze und Reden* (Munich, 1963), pp. 36 ff. Cf. also by the same author the article "Scholasticism" in the *Encyclopedia Britannica* (1972 edition).
[4] Mal 2:15.
[5] *Ibid.*
[6] II, II, 142; 153, 3 ad 3.
[7] Karl Barth, *Kirchliche Dogmatik* IV, 2, p. 844.
[8] *Phaedrus* 228 a.
[9] *Ibid.*, 243 c 1.
[10] *Ibid.*, 243 c 2.
[11] *Dichtung und Wahrheit*, Part One, Book 5.

[12] Rollo May, *Love and Will*, p. 57.

[13] *The Clown*, chap. 7.

[14] Erich Fromm, *The Art of Loving*, pp. 45 f.

[15] Joachim Bodamer, *Liebe und Eros in der modernen Welt* (Hamburg, 1958), p. 40. In an essay "Ich und Du," published as long ago as 1925, Martin Buber says, "If we deduct from the much-discussed eroticism of the age everything that is essentially egotistic, that is, all relationships in which one is not present to the other, not summoned to mind by him, so that the one is only enjoying himself — what would be left?" *Werke*, vol. I (Munich-Heidelberg, 1962), p. 108.

[16] Paul Ricoeur, *Sexualität. Wunder — Abwege — Rätsel*. Rischer Bücherei (Frankfurt, 1967), p. 15.

[17] Rollo May, *Love and Will*, p. 282.

[18] Seymour L. Halleck, "The Roots of Student Despair." In *Think* (published by IBM), vol. 33 (1967), p. 22.

[19] Jean Brun in Ricoeur, *Sexualität*, p. 129.

[20] Rollo May, *Love and Will*, p. 40.

[21] To Zelter, March 18, 1811.

[22] Paul Ricoeur, *Sexualität*, p. 16.

[23] Gerald Sykes, *The Cool Millennium* (New York, 1967). Cited in Rollo May, *Love and Will*, p. 59.

[24] *Ibid.*

[25] *Die Sehnsucht nach dem ganz Anderen* (Hamburg, 1970), p. 74.

[26] I am speaking here of the "pill" only to the extent that it is a means for making sex-consumption easy. The extremely complicated problem of birth control and family planning would, of course, involve far more discussion.

[27] Joachim Bodamer, *Sexualitat und Liebe* (Hamburg, 1970), p. 20.

[28] Bodamer, *Liebe und Eros*, p. 40.

[29] *Ibid.*, p. 35.

[30] *Kirchliche Dogmatik* III, 4, p. 148.

[31] For example, the entry "Exorcismus" (and also "Satan" and "Teufel") does not appear in the German theological dictionary (*Kleines theologisches Wörterbuch*) edited by Karl Rahner and Herbert Vorgrimler (Freiburg, 1961).

[32] Harvey Cox, *The Secular City* (New York: Macmillan, 1965), p. 192.

[33] Cyrill Koupernik in Paul Ricoeur, *Sexualität*, p. 246.

[34] Rollo May, *Love and Will*, p. 317.

[35] *The Poems of John Donne*, ed. Sir H. J. C. Grierson (London: Oxford University Press, 1933), p. 317.

[36] Harvey Cox, *loc. cit.*

[37] Sophistes 236 ff. Cf. also Josef Pieper, *Missbrauch der Sprache—Missbrauch der Macht*, pp. 36 f.

[38] According to the report in the *Frankfurter Allgemeine Zeitung* (September 6, 1969) on the Teenage Fair in Düsseldorf, the ad-

vertising slogan of a furniture factory there read: "Make your table sexy and youthful."

[39] *Studies in Words,* pp. 298 f.

[40] This is a compression of the Platonic text and therefore not quite literal, but it is, I think, a faithful rendering of the meaning of a passage in the *Politeia* (492 b – 493 a).

X

[1] *Nicomachean Ethics* 8, 4; 1156 b.

[2] Cf. the illuminating chapter entitled Friendship in C. S. Lewis's *The Four Loves.*

[3] R. W. Emerson, Essays (first series), "Friendship," p. 151.

[4] II, II, 27, 1.

[5] Erich Fromm, *The Art of Loving,* p. 35.

[6] *Ibid.,* p. 37.

[7] In January 1971 Pope Paul VI made her the first recipient of the John XXIII Peace Prize, which had been founded in 1963.

[8] *Eros und Agape* I, p. 31.

[9] The magnificent formulation that agape is essentially "lost love" comes from Anders Nygren, who in support of it quotes Luther's phrase, *amoris est falli. Eros und Agape* II, p. 554.

[10] Thomas Aquinas, *In duo praecepta;* no. 1134. *Opuscula Theologica* II (Turin, 1954).

[11] *Ibid.,* no. 1150.

[12] *Dilectio caritatis sub se comprehendit omnes dilectiones humanas.* Car. 7.

[13] Perfection presupposes perfectibility; cf. I, 2, 2 ad 1.

[14] Cf. Josef Pieper, *Happiness and Contemplation* (New York, 1958), pp. 39 ff.

[15] Augustine, Serm. 21, 2; Migne, *Patrologia Latina* 38, 143.

[16] *Caritas non est qualiscumque amor Dei, sed amor Dei quo diligitur ut beatitudinis objectum.* I, II, 65, 5 ad 1. *Diligendus est ex caritate Deus ut radix beatitudinis.* Car. 7.

[17] Car. 4 ad 2.

[18] Car. 7; II, II, 25, 5 ad 2.

[19] Car. 7.

[20] Perf. vit. spir., cap. 2.

[21] Car. 7.

[22] C. S. Lewis, *They Asked for a Paper,* p. 210.

[23] *Deus qui humanae substantiae dignitatem mirabiliter condidisti et mirabilius reformasti* . . . —such is the wording of a prayer in the "oldest books of the Roman Mass" which has recently been deleted from the Ordo Missae. Cf. J. A. Jungmann, *Missarum Solemnia* (Vienna, 1948), vol. I, pp. 77 ff.

[24] Cf. I, 1, 8 ad 2; 62, 5; I, II, 99, 2 ad 1; III, 71, 1 ad 1.

[25] In Ps 121, 12. Migne, *Patrologia Latina* 37, 1628.

[26] In Isa., cap. 30.